DATE DUE			
OCT 1 0 199 RET			

THE
ENROLLMENT
EXPLOSION

THE ENROLLMENT EXPLOSION

 A Half-Century of Attendance

in U.S. Colleges and Universities

BY GARLAND G. PARKER

Vice Provost for Admissions and Records and Professor of History
and Educational Research, University of Cincinnati

School & Society Books • New York • 1971

To

RAYMOND WALTERS

pioneer enrollment analyst,
enthusiastic scholar,
prominent educator

and

WALTER CONSUELO LANGSAM

eminent historian,
able administrator,
wise counselor

whose efforts as successive University of Cincinnati
presidents made this study of enrollments possible

✦ CONTENTS

✦ PREFACE

THE 1969-70 ACADEMIC YEAR marked the end of a tumultuous decade, an epochal half-century, and the 50th anniversary of the publication in *School & Society* of the annual collegiate enrollment reports. These reports, initiated in 1919-20 by Dr. Raymond Walters, president emeritus of the University of Cincinnati, have been prepared by the undersigned since 1960-61. A new chapter of our national history opened with the 1919-20 school year. In turn, 1969-70 served as a crossing point into the critical decade of the 1970's, when some decisions basic to the future of the nation were pending. In reporting student and teacher numbers as well as interpreting trends and events in higher education, the *School & Society* studies comprise a unique source document and one of the few continuous statistical and narrative accounts spanning that significant 50-year period.

It appeared academically justifiable, urgent, and even compelling to use this record as a prime source for a historical account by decades that would give an overview of national events, define some major trends in higher education, and interrelate these developments with the story of collegiate enrollments. Too often, the story of higher education in the U.S. has been written and studied as a parallel current to, or even as an eddy isolated from, the mainstream of history. Unquestionably, with student numbers approaching eight millions, burgeoning budgets, physical facilities under strain, unrest and activism in student life that closed many universities in 1970,

9

and with so many vital problems of the future dependent upon solutions that must derive in the main from college campuses, higher education must be considered and studied as one of the major elements in the national scene. Thus, an objective here is to show the interrelationship of educational events to other facets of our national development.

The fact that this volume is based upon the only continuous report series tabulating students and teachers as well as providing interpretive commentary over the 50-year period under review gives it a uniqueness that should contribute to its value as a textbook and a reference in graduate and undergraduate courses in many academic disciplines. It is hoped that it will be particularly useful as a reference work in the general field of higher education and helpful to users in college, university, private, and public libraries.

A cherished prerogative of the author is to acknowledge the indispensable support he has received from others in the publication of this volume as well as in the preparation since 1960-61 of the annual *School & Society* collegiate enrollment reports. Collectively, these publications have comprised a mammoth enterprise that never could have been completed without such aid.

Space precludes any detailed coverage of the outstanding intellectual and educational achievements of Dr. Raymond Walters, who assumed authorship of the annual reports in 1919-20 and continued them for 40 years, through 1959-60. Some facts of his professional experience are recounted later, but it may be noted here that he was an internationally recognized authority on college and university administration as well as collegiate enrollments upon his retirement from the presidency of the University of Cincinnati on Aug. 31, 1955, at the age of 70. He was the holder of 14 honorary degrees, the author of hundreds of scholarly articles, seven books, and was a Fellow in the American Association for the Advancement of Science. His 40 annual survey articles and his published review in 1960 of developments over four decades of U.S. collegiate enrollments have been of inestimable value to this author. In addition, the writer recalls with pleasure his own experience as a faculty member under the presidential leadership of that able man. It has been a pleasure and an honor to continue the research and reports initiated by Dr. Walters. To his sons, Raymond, Everett, and Philip, as well as their families, the author likewise is appreciative for sympathy and support since 1960, and expresses the hope that this volume will serve as a fitting tribute to their father for his work as a statistician in higher education. Dr. Walters passed away on Oct. 25, 1970.

To Dr. Walter C. Langsam, inaugurated as president of the University of Cincinnati in 1955, the author acknowledges an incalculable debt of gratitude as a personal mentor and a professional sponsor. It was Pres. Langsam who assured the writer in 1960 that he could and should assume the responsibility for the annual *School & Society* enrollment reports, pursuant to the illness that rendered it impossible for Dr. Walters to continue his work. In later years, Pres. Langsam and the Board of Directors of the University of Cincinnati made available the financial and staff support essential to the production of the annual enrollment studies and the preparation of the manuscript of this volume. Pres. Langsam's personal interest, continued encouragement, his own national stature as an eminent historian, and his wide reputation as a university administrator have contributed significantly to any success the author has enjoyed over the years. At the vice-presidential level, the writer also acknowledges the invaluable support of Ralph C. Bursiek, Hoke S. Greene, and Thomas N. Bonner in their roles, successively, as his immediate superiors. Similarly, to John P. DeCamp, Frank Heck, Richard B. Baker, and Joyce Garn Agnew, for their effective services as public information officers, the writer is greatly indebted.

Mrs. Robert R. Stillwell, who first began to work with Dr. Walters in 1941 and who has shared responsibility for the reports since 1960 with this writer, merits especial tribute. Her preparation of the enrollment tables, competence in statistical computation, and expert professional advice have been of prime importance. To Mr. and Mrs. Stillwell and to their son and daughter, James and Kathryn, all of whom have shared in various aspects of the tabular preparations, and whose personal and family schedules have been interrupted on numerous occasions, both by day and night, as a result of intrusions of business related to the reports, the writer always will be indebted. In respect to correspondence, manuscript typing, and communication by telephone and telegraph with reporting and press officers across the nation, the writer recognizes the able assistance of Lynn M. Barber, Anita Bernstein, Donna Ferneding, and Lois Whitenack. ·

The writer can not overemphasize the personal, editorial, and administrative support and encouragement he has received from William W. Brickman, editor; Stanley Lehrer, president and publisher; and Robert S. Rothenberg, vice-president for circulation, respectively, of the Society for the Advancement of Education, which publishes *School & Society*. It should be noted that this important public service venture of publishing the annual collegiate enrollment report for many years past has been made possible only by significant subsidy support from *School & Society* and the University of Cincinnati.

It is a pleasure, also, to acknowledge the generous cooperation of thousands of registrars and other statistical officers who each year have supplied the indispensable data for the annual reports. Appreciation is expressed to the successive presidents and executive committee members of the American Association of Collegiate Registrars and Admissions Officers for their counsel and encouragement. Similarly, to the press and other media representatives, the author extends thanks for the wide national and international coverage that annually has been extended to the *School & Society* collegiate enrollment reports.

A final tribute is reserved for the author's wife, Elizabeth, his daughters, Hope Parker Brandenburgh and Anne Parker Colter, and their husbands. Since 1960, work on the enrollment studies and this volume has usurped the time that otherwise could have been devoted to wedding anniversaries, Thanksgiving and Christmas holidays, and many other occasions throughout the year. To his own parents, Mr. and Mrs. Clarence Parker, and to his brothers, Allen and Norman, there also is a sentimental debt that never can be discharged.

GARLAND G. PARKER

Cincinnati, Ohio
August, 1970

 INTRODUCTION

Fifty Years in Minuscule

THE HALF-CENTURY spanned by the *School & Society* collegiate enrollment reports well may have been the most dynamic time segment in the history of mankind, in a secular sense at least. Not one, but many, revolutions have been wrought in this exciting, productive, and dangerous age. In agriculture, the resort to large-scale farming by machine effected a revolution in food production and the organization of society, both rural and urban. In the realm of science, not even the sky has been the limit. Movement in exploration from the earth to the moon and from the molecule to the atom reflects the high scientific adventure of these dramatic years. The transition from silent movie to television, radio to radar, hard cover to paperback, dirt road to superhighway, phonograph to stereo, and typewriter to computer only illustrate the tremendous changes that mark this half-century. Problems have mounted along with progress. The aftermath of one World War, the waging of another, limited international conflicts in the last two decades, and efforts to cope with depression, affluence, poverty, pollution, and racism all indicate the problems that still challenge the ingenuity of man. Truly, in terms of knowledge, progress, population, problems, and conflict, this has been a volatile half-century. The impact of its combined pressures upon higher education has produced a veritable explosion in collegiate enrollments. An increasingly vital role in the determination of our national destiny has been played by the escalating numbers of students in our institutions of higher education. The tremendous forces of this enrollment explosion should be directed and controlled in ways that will permit the vast energies and ideas of the college coterie to be applied constructively to the leadership of the nation and the solution of its pressing problems. The contributions of college attendees in the last 50 years have been notable, but much more will be required of them in the years ahead.

The annual reports from 1919-20 through 1969-70 published by *School & Society* provide statistical and narrative records, unavailable elsewhere, on which to base a review of collegiate enrollment developments and their implications in those years. The perspective of a half-century provided by this analysis should be meaningful in the years ahead.

In the Beginning

In 1919, Raymond Walters accepted the invitation of J. McKeen Cattell[1] to assume responsibility for the collegiate enrollment studies that for some years had been published in *Science* and later in *School & Society*. Experience as a teacher of English and registrar at Lehigh University, 1911-21, provided Dr. Walters with an excellent apprenticeship for the assignment. Later responsibilities as a teacher of English and dean at Swarthmore College, 1921-32, and president of the University of Cincinnati, 1932-55, reflected not only his own professional development, but also his growing competence as the master of the *School & Society* enrollment reports. By the time he had completed his 40th annual study in 1959-60, he had acquired a national reputation as "Statistician Laureate of Higher Education." In 1960, this writer[2] assumed responsibility for the reports.

Structure of the School & Society Reports

In the use of, and reference to, the *School & Society* studies, it is

---

[1] Distinguished psychologist, founder, and long-time editor of *Science* (1894-1944) and of *School & Society* (1915-39).

[2] Teacher of history and English in secondary schools, 1937-45; graduate assistant and fellow in European history, University of Wisconsin, 1946-48; assistant and associate professor of history, 1948-66, professor of history and educational research since 1967, appointed registrar in 1956, dean of admissions and university registrar, 1964-67, and, since 1967, vice provost for admissions and records, University of Cincinnati.

important to understand what they are purported to be and what they are not. When Dr. Walters took over the reports in 1919, they covered only 30 large universities designated by Cattell that usually were described as "neither the thirty largest . . . nor necessarily the leading institutions" in the country, but they were "representative."[3] This, of course, was only enrollment-taking by sample, and was not acceptable to the standards the new author set for himself and for the institutions of higher education to be covered in the reports. Important changes soon came that greatly improved the studies as statistical instruments and bases for interpreting significant trends in collegiate enrollments. Dr. Walters continued to report on the 30 "representative" institutions for many years in considerable detail, but, in his third annual report, for 1921-22, he expanded the total number of institutions surveyed to 123 of the 150 four-year colleges and universities then on the approved list of the Association of American Universities. This still was far short of complete coverage of all the colleges and universities in the country, but it added breadth and significance to the annual studies. By 1929-30, there were 226 institutions comprehended in the annual report. In the 1930-34 period, the institutions included on an American Council on Education list were surveyed. This extended the survey to the 431 institutions then listed as "approved" by five regional associations. The American Council publication was discontinued, and from 1936-56 the studies were based on a similar list issued by the Council on Medical Education of the American Medical Association. It included universities and four-year colleges approved by the regional associations. Since 1957, the directory issued on behalf of the National Committee of Regional Accrediting Agencies (now the Federation of Regional Accrediting Agencies of Higher Education) has been used as a guide for including schools in the annual reports. Reports on junior or two-year colleges intermittently have been included since 1933-34, usually on the basis of special communications from the American Association of Junior Colleges. Beginning in 1960, this writer made it clear in the definitions that enrollment data for the two-year programs, branches, or colleges administered by the four-year institutions should be included in the enrollments of the parent schools. The *School & Society* report, thus, eventually earned the distinction of being the only annual study that covered the accred-

---

[3] Raymond Walters, "Statistics of Registration for Thirty Universities for 1918 and 1919," *School & Society*, 12:294, Aug. 14, 1920, p. 109.

ited universities, senior colleges, four-year colleges, and the two-year units administered by institutions in the first three categories. From the 30 institutions surveyed in 1919, the study has grown so that, by 1969-70, inclusive of late responses, reports were received from 1,167 accredited schools.

Another characteristic of this series has been its emphasis upon the differentiation between full-time and part-time students. In the second Walters report, for 1920-21, institutions were asked to indicate separate counts for the two categories. In 1932-33, the device of classifying institutions of higher education and their enrollments by the following types was introduced: universities and large institutions of complex organization, with separate tables for those under public control and those under private control; independent colleges of arts and sciences; and other independent institutions—technological schools and teachers colleges. This classification was in pursuance of the advice of a committee of the Association of American Colleges. In 1957-58, other classifications under accredited independent institutions added were fine arts, applied arts and music, and theological seminaries and schools for lay workers.

The tabulation of freshman enrollment data by selected subject matter categories also has been an earmark of these studies since 1934-35. At first, full-time freshmen were tallied in four undergraduate fields: liberal arts (later referred to as arts and sciences), engineering, commerce (or business administration), and agriculture. Teacher training (later referred to as education), in 1939, and nursing, in 1961, were added to the freshman groups. In the latter year, also, a conglomerate "all others" category was designed to sweep up all freshmen in other disciplines or those who were undecided or unidentifiable as to their majors.

Still another facet of the *School & Society* enrollment tables has been the demographical one. Despite earlier and occasional references and charts, it was not until 1934-35 that a geographical table was introduced into the report as a regular feature. It now includes the following regions: New England, Middle Atlantic, East North Central, West North Central, South Atlantic, East South Central, West South Central, Mountain, Pacific, and Territorial.

A final tabulation field in the reports has been for teachers. As inherited by Dr. Walters, the report presented data on "teachers and officers." As early as 1920-21, Dr. Walters was seeking to differentiate between teaching and administrative staff. The evolution was toward an identification of full-time teachers as those who taught half-time or more and the rest, provided they did teach, as part-time teachers; both groups were included in the grand totals.

In his review of *Four Decades of U.S. Collegiate Enrollments,* published in 1960, Dr. Walters stated the definitions under which institutions were asked to report their enrollments in 1920-21 as follows: "The full-time regular student is one who has completed a four-year high-school course and is devoting his main time and attention during the collegiate year to study in a curriculum leading to a degree.

"The part-time student is a student whose main time and attention are given to some other employment and who takes courses of full college and university standard in the late afternoon, evening, and Saturday classes."[4] The definitions used for the 50th anniversary report in 1969-70 reflected the increasing comprehensiveness and sophistication in these studies over a half-century.[5] The criterion of 12-or-more credit hours of class attendance per week for identifying full-time students first was stated by Dr. Walters in the report for 1927-28. This figure was standardized by the Veterans Administration for World War II undergraduate veterans receiving full benefits, with 14 hours later specified for Korean veterans. The National Collegiate Athletic Association also has required 12 hours for student eligibility in intercollegiate athletics. In recent years, 12 hours has remained the basic standard on the presumption that this does amount to 75% or more of a normal program for undergraduates, but it has been understood that the load may be less for graduate students.

Diplomacy and Pressure

Early in the Walters series, there were problems involving the pollster and the responding institutions. It is ironic, but no doubt reflective of human nature, as well as practical problems in many cases, that some institutions, or their reporting officers, are reluctant to provide enrollment information requested of them. Some of the original 30 schools included in the survey found it difficult to comply with Walters' request for differentiation between full-time and part-time students. As a result, in 1921-22, no less distinguished an

---

[4] Raymond Walters, *Four Decades of U.S. Collegiate Enrollments* (New York: Society for the Advancement of Education, 1960), p. 1.

[5] Garland G. Parker, "Statistics of Attendance in American Universities and Colleges, 1969-70," *School & Society,* 98:2322, January, 1970, pp. 41-58.

institution than New York University was dropped from coveted membership in the original group of 30 institutions surveyed and was replaced by the University of Washington as a "representative" school from another area. On many occasions, Dr. Walters refused to use data that did not meet the specifications. That he was no amateur in the diplomacy of higher education is reflected by his securing, in 1922, the endorsement of his definitions of enrollment categories by the American Association of Collegiate Registrars.[6] For many years thereafter, he cited this agreement in support of his annual requests for data from the colleges and universities. The need for understanding and finesse in relations with the responding schools has continued to the present time. Academic rivalries among some institutions that seem petty in retrospect often have complicated the preparation of the reports. In the early 1960's, heavy pressure was exerted upon this author to drop the series and rely solely thereafter upon reports issued by the U.S. Office of Education. The writer, the University of Cincinnati, and *School & Society* persevered in the conviction that a national collegiate enrollment report prepared responsibly in semi-private channels provided an important informational and interpretive service in the field of higher education that should be maintained. That such pressure has disappeared in recent years is reassuring, and the writer expresses his heartfelt appreciation to the many hundreds of institutions and reporting officers who willingly and cooperatively provide the indispensable data for the annual reports.

In this book, consideration will be given to a decennial review of enrollments, certain features that transcend all 50 years, the two-year college movement, current crossing points in higher education, and a look ahead into the decade of the 1970's. The historian seldom poses as a prophet, but his work may be helpful in the future. It is hoped that this book will be of aid to all, but especially to administrators, admissions officers, registrars, and faculty, in detecting trends as well as in analyzing and solving problems confronting higher education. This study suggests the need to project enrollments and anticipate their impact. Population data and other factors indicate for the 1970's a deceleration in enrollment increases, an oversupply of teachers and other highly trained specialists, and a standstill or even declining enrollment in the early 1980's. Advance planning for these and other

---

[6] Raymond Walters, "The Scope of Collegiate Registration Statistics," *School & Society*, 16:399, Aug. 19, 1922, pp. 201-203.

eventualities may be facilitated by this book.

Many factors examined in the book are indicative of trends and problems. Some of these are college-age attendance, classification of schools and students, freshman enrollments, proportionate enrollment of women to men, coeducation, role and survival of private colleges, veterans' education, multiversities, unitary state systems, and urbanism. The need is indicated for close attention to faculty and student concerns and pressures and for emphasis upon good teaching and a meaningful student-teacher relationship. Finally, the book demonstrates that community, state, national, and even international events interact with campus developments more than ever before, probably will continue to do so, and must be taken into account in future planning for higher education.

THE
ENROLLMENT
EXPLOSION

1. The 1920's and the Ivory Tower

Collegians in a Tempestuous Decade

Dr. WALTERS' first enrollment report opened with the observation that, in the 1919-20 academic year, a "great number of young men who left in 1917 and 1918 for service in the war" [World War I, then referred to as The Great War] returned to American colleges and universities. As a result, enrollments totaling 147,274 students in the 30 institutions surveyed were far larger in most cases than ever before. Those institutions had lost 17.7% of their enrollments in 1917, but, by 1919, their combined registrations showed a gain of 47% over 1914. As was to be demonstrated repeatedly in later decades, military service undoubtedly had alerted veterans to the value and need of college training and stimulated their re-enrollments, as well as initial entry, into college. The educational and financial implications of the rapid rise in enrollments was alluded to in a report from the University of Wisconsin: "The return to peace, with the accompanying rush of students and mounting costs of all kinds, has brought about at Wisconsin, as in many other universities, a situation which can only be described as a crisis.' "[7]

As the impact of the war receded in the early 1920's, other characteristics of a somewhat tempestuous decade asserted themselves. This was the time for a "return to normalcy" in foreign and domestic affairs. The U.S. turned its back on the League of Nations and pursued a policy of isolation, except on issues and places—in Latin America and the Far East, for example—where national interests directly were involved. Tax reduction, tariff increases, immigration restrictions, emphasis upon economy, and free enterprise were the modes of the time. The business community generally enjoyed prosperity, but the farmers suffered declining prices after the war, and later were hurt by the loss of markets abroad as a result of the imposition of quotas on American agricultural commodities by foreign countries in retaliation against the high tariffs on their own goods. As the decade wore on, business leaders and many other citizens indulged in a frenzy of speculation on the stock market that culminated in the great crash in the autumn of 1929.

On the social side, the so-called "Roaring Twenties" were noted for a marked rise in crime and gangsterism as a result, in part, of the opportunities for illegal gains from the liquor trade made possible by prohibition. In pursuance of the war and its aftermath, there was a general relaxation of former standards in respect to dress, social customs, and relations between the sexes. Women in the urban areas, at least, moved quickly to take advantage of the perquisites bestowed upon them by an increasing emancipation that pertained not only to matters of suffrage, sex, and dress, but also to education and job opportunity. The American public developed a voracious appetite for literature at all levels, as well as a rising interest in music, both jazz and classical. Legitimate theater waned, but the motion picture and radio businesses boomed.[8]

Against this background of obvious concern with things material, it is important to recognize that an increasingly high value was placed upon education. In 1919-20, there were some 597,880 degree-credit students enrolled in American colleges and universities, but by 1929-30 that number had increased to 1,100,737. In 1919-20, there were 1,041 institutions of higher education in the U.S., and by

---

[7] Walters, "Statistics of Registration of Thirty Universities for 1918 and 1919," *loc. cit.*

[8] Walter Consuelo Langsam, *World History Since 1870* (New York: American Book Co., 1963), pp. 324-331.

1929-30 the number was 1,409.[9] There was a strong feeling among parents generally, especially immigrants, that educational advancement offered a sure outlet from ghetto life and a highroad to success for their children. The colleges largely were populated by the off-spring of the well-to-do, but many thousands of lower-middle-class students from urban, as well as rural, areas found their way onto college campuses. The nation was on the threshold of the greatest experiment in mass education at the collegiate level that the world yet had seen. These were the years before the imposition of highly selective admissions standards, as well as limited enrollments, in many colleges, and fees in the state-supported and land-grant schools were low. The flapper psychology and the raccoon coat syndrome were among the external earmarks of the college set in the 1920's, but these concepts oversimplify the situation. There was a more serious approach to higher education than the superficial signs of the times imply. Indeed, from the vantage point of the 1960's—so marked by pressures, overcrowding, and dissent—one may view in a wistful mood a quieter time when the "ivory tower" concept was more valid than it ever was to be again. Although much attention was given to the humanities and the liberal arts in collegiate education in this decade, the emphasis upon professional and technical education was significant. The Walters reports provided a wealth of information dealing with education in medicine, dentistry, engineering, law, business administration (commerce), and agriculture, especially in the 30 schools subject to detailed consideration in the early studies.

Enrollment Panorama in the 1920's

With the above observations as a frame of reference, further enrollment developments in the 1920's may be noted. In 1920-21, Dr. Walters reported a grand total of 207,407 students in the 30 institutions surveyed, as compared with 183,459 in 1919-20;[10] this represented an increase of 13%. Full-time totals for 29 of the 30 schools reporting were fewer by 3,805 than for 1919-20, but this seeming decline may have reflected discrepancies in the differentiation be-

---

[9] U.S. Office of Education, *Digest of Educational Statistics, 1968* (Washington, D.C.: U.S. Government Printing Office, 1968), p. 69.

[10] The data in Table I of the 1919-20 report comprise a grand total of 183,459, but 183,620 in Table III.

tween full-time and part-time students that the author was insisting upon for the first time. In 1921-22, the study was expanded to include reports from 123 institutions on the "approved" list of the Association of American Universities. The grand total enrollment for these institutions was 366,608. In the 30 selected schools for which comparable data were available, there was a seven per cent increase in full-time enrollment and a 17% increase in grand total enrollment. By 1922-23, the postwar enrollment rise flattened out a bit when full-time enrollments in 123 comparable institutions, among 140 reporting, rose only two per cent, but, even so, the grand total count was up by 14%. This same report called attention to the fact that, by 1922-23, in 29 of the 30 representative schools, full-time students had increased 56% and grand total students by 87% in five years; the respective totals in these schools for 1922-23 were 149,064 and 232,577. By 1923-24, enrollment gains—three per cent for full-time and six per cent for grand total counts—had reverted to the normal prewar increase rates. Nevertheless, the author observed that the numerical growth at some of the larger state universities exceeded what formerly would have been a typical enrollment "in an old New England college." In 1924-25, the full-time increase was 8.5% and the grand total increased 4.6%. The full-time student total in 160 reporting colleges was 308,785. Again, in 1925-26, full-time students showed a sharp rise of seven per cent, and the grand total number increased by 4.8%. The highwater increase marks of the 1920's were made in 1926-27, with an 11% increase in full-time and nine per cent in grand total students in the 178 comparable reporting schools. In the 1927-28 report, percentage increases were cited on a five-year basis. In 211 reporting institutions, the 410,712 full-time students showed an increase of 25% over the 328,883 tabulated in 1922.

In retrospect, the 1928-29 report is especially interesting. That study revealed "the smallest annual increase since the war," as reflected in data from 216 institutions in the U.S. and Canada. The 417,526 full-time students showed an increase of just over two per cent. Possible causes listed for the enrollment slowdown were agricultural and industrial conditions, junior college developments, migration of students to the large universities, enrollment limitations in some schools, and immigration restrictions. Also, U.S. Bureau of Education birthrate and infant mortality figures indicated that only 20 children per thousand of the population reached one year of age in 1926, as compared to 22.5 in 1916. The speculation was that school and college enrollments soon would reach stationary levels, if these conditions continued. Enrollments in the closing year of the decade, 1929-30, may have been affected by incipient depression conditions, in view of the low 1.5% increase in full-time and two per cent increase in grand total students reported by 226 institutions. The stock market crash, in October, 1929, came after the opening of the colleges in the fall; the 1929-30 report was published on Dec. 14, 1929. It is curious that the author made no mention of the deteriorating economic situation that was to have such an impact upon the nation as a whole, as well as its educational system. Undoubtedly, time had not been sufficient yet to provide a perspective on the events of that troubled season.

2. Depression and College in the 1930's

The National Scene

THE MAJOR MOVEMENTS in national life that constituted strong conditioning influences upon higher education in the decade of the 1930's are worth a summary. There is no question but that the pallor of economic depression discolored the basic backdrop of the higher education stage. From 1929 to 1933, the nation's economy declined at a precipitate rate. Unemployment that once mounted to over 13,000,000 persons, deflation of the dollar that approximated 40%, and an increase of the national debt by over 50% were signs of the mid-1930's. Traditional policies for restoring prosperity that always seemed just "around the corner" in the Republican administration of Pres. Herbert Hoover, 1929-33, were ineffective. With the inception of the Democratic administration of Franklin D. Roosevelt and his New Deal in 1933, a series of radical new measures were adopted to fight depression and promote prosperity. These involved Federal work programs for the unemployed, placing a floor under wages in many industries, pro-labor legislation, the passage of the first Social Security Act, payments to farmers for crop reduction and soil conservation, and Federal subsidies for needy college students. The rise of Nazism in Germany and Fascism in Italy produced a pall of impending war in Europe that increasingly enveloped the U.S. in the later years of the decade. Anti-war sentiment was strong, and many young men averred they never again would fight in a foreign conflict. There was rising social concern over the fact that one-third of the nation's population allegedly was "ill-housed, ill-clad, ill-nourished." Many voices rose to question the "system," and educational communities harbored increasing numbers of outspoken liberals. It came to be expected that the government should assume a more active role in promoting prosperity, social welfare, and regulating industry. The prime goal of most persons was economic security, marriages were delayed, the birthrate declined, and jobs were scarce throughout the decade. There were fads, such as the Lindy dance craze and goldfish-swallowing episodes. The decade has been dubbed "the great band era" in the field of music. Radio was in its heyday, and offered the country a wide range of quality programs of entertainment, music, sports, and news. It was generally a conservative era in dress and in respect to the social amenities. The repeal of Prohibition in 1933 and the reappearance of legal liquor in many communities had important economic, as well as social, implications. Crime continued to be a problem, and the era was noted for the further rise of gangsterism.

Enrollment Ups and Downs

In the light of this background, what were the developments in collegiate enrollments? That the Depression was an omnipresent factor in higher education is evidenced by the considerable attention given to it in the annual Walters reports. In general, collegiate enrollments held their own or even continued to increase through the early Depression years, 1929-1931; fell off noticeably in 1932-33 and 1933-34; rose significantly in the next two years; and maintained an upward trend throughout the remainder of the decade. Some generalizations may be offered in explanation of these increase-decrease trends. Unquestionably, despite the throes of the Depression, the American people continued to have faith in higher education as a stepping-stone to success for themselves and their children. Even though times got harder, every effort was made to support their sons, especially, in school as long as financial resources permitted. Also, since jobs were scarce, it was better for young people to be in college than to remain idle. In 1932-33 and 1933-34, after savings were dissipated, the Depression had reached its depth, and few relief measures yet had become effective, it was inevitable that enrollments should decline. In later years, significant Federal aid to needy college students, coupled with somewhat more prosperous economic conditions, again made enrollment increases possible.

The tenacity with which collegians pursued arts and sciences curricula in good times and bad in the 1930's is remarkable. They were considered preparatory for many professions and also for the good life. In the early depression years, enrollments in engineering, technical, vocational, teacher education, journalism, music, and pharmacy courses declined, but revived with the return of prosperity. Engineering boomed in the middle and later years of the decade, in reflection of economic improvement and the rising need for technical talent in defense preparations. In the same period, Dr. Walters emphasized that the birthrate figures suggested a leveling-off of the population by mid-century, and viewed with much concern the impact this would have on higher education. In kindergarten and the first five elementary grades, it was observed that, with 14,151,135 pupils in attendance, there was a decrease of 7.7% from 1925-26 to 1935-36. This seeming human shortage and the impact of World War II were to have shattering effects at the college level in the 1940's. In the long run, however, the increasing rate of college-age attendance and the resurgence of the birthrate were factors that would be productive of booming enrollments in the late 1950's and the 1960's. The year-to-year enrollment developments now may be reviewed.

In 1930-31, a full-time total of 587,671 students in 431 institutions were reported, for a gain of 3.5%, and the grand total increased to 867,226, one per cent higher than 1929. The smaller grand total rise was attributed to losses in summer school registrants, then included in the grand total counts, incidental no doubt to depression factors. The next year, 1931-32, enrollments over-all barely surpassed the record totals of the previous year with a 0.6% increase in full-time students and a loss of 0.5% in the grand total count. By 1932-33, however, the depression was taking its toll, with declines of seven per cent in grand total enrollment and 4.5% in full-time students. The enrollment decrease in the four-year schools was explained in part by increased attendance in junior colleges and the fact that some students were taking postgraduate high school courses. Full-time enrollments in comparable schools went down another five per cent in 1933-34, while the grand total figure declined by nine per cent. The latter decrease was attributed largely to a 23% drop in summer session students in the large universities. The respective full-time and grand total numbers were 607,251 and 888,017 in 546 institutions.

Federal Aid Programs—NYA

Enrollment rises resumed in 1934-35, when 655,725 full-time students in 567 institutions showed an increase of five per cent and grand total registrants rose by 7.5%. The freshman table, incorporated into the study that year for the first time, revealed 155,212 students—comprehending four subject-matter areas—in 487 comparable reporting schools, for a sharp increase of 14%. That was the year in which financial aid from the Federal Emergency Relief Administration (FERA) first became available for financially needy students with character and ability. In 1935-36, this program came under the National Youth Administration, and was referred to as the NYA. It remained in force throughout the decade and, by 1939, average payments of $15 per month for work performed by undergraduates and $30 per month for graduate students were allowed. In 1934-35, there were 94,331 NYA students working in 1,466 institutions, and by 1937-38 the number was 145,778 in 1,665 colleges. In 1936, about 12% of the full-time students were earning part of their way through college on this program; in 1939, the percentage was 10%. It was expected that NYA students would be assigned to "socially desirable work, including the sort customarily done in the institution by students who are working their way through college, such as clerical, library, and research work." The program also was intended to "provide unique educational and socially useful opportunities which would in many cases supplement a student's classroom activities." As one whose undergraduate education was facilitated by NYA work opportunities, the writer can testify to the soundness of the program in its support of thousands of students who otherwise could not have attended college. From the vantage point of 1970, a sum of $15 per month, or $0.30 per hour, seems paltry, but it was significant in the student economy of the 1930's. In view of the current emphasis upon educational opportunity for disadvantaged students from various ethnic minorities, the following statement in 1936 from an official government bulletin is of interest: " 'Negro graduate students who

cannot be cared for within a particular institution's quota for graduate aid, after it has made a fair allocation for Negro graduates from
its regular quota, may apply for the special Negro Graduate Aid
Fund.' "[11]

Enrollments in the Late 1930's

The percentage increase of 700,730 full-time students in 577
schools in 1935-36 was 6.6% more than 1934-35; and 1,063,472, an
eight per cent increase, was the grand total—the first time that
1,000,000 students were counted in the accredited schools. The freshman increase was 7.4%. In 1936-37, the freshman, full-time, and
grand total increases, respectively, were 4.7%, 6.5%, and 7.3%. In
1937-38, despite a one-third reduction in Federal aid to needy students, full-time enrollees in 602 institutions increased by 3.6%; grand
total, by four per cent; and freshmen, in the areas tabulated, by
0.4%. In 1938-39, the increases were 6.6% for full-time, 6.8% for
grand total, and 4.4% for freshman students. At the close of the
decade, in 1939-40, in 648 institutions, there were 873,697 full-time
and 1,323,874 grand total students, for respective increases of 2.7%
and 1.2%. It is perhaps a reflection of the mood of the time that no
mention was made in this report of the gathering clouds of war,
despite the fact that World War II already had been precipitated by
the invasion of Poland by Nazi Germany under Adolf Hitler on
Sept. 1, 1939.

---

[11] Raymond Walters, "Statistics of Registration in American Universities and
Colleges, 1935," *School & Society*, 42:1094, Dec. 14, 1935, pp. 801-819;
Raymond Walters, "Statistics of Registration in American Universities and Col-
leges, 1936," *School & Society*, 44:1147, Dec. 19, 1936, pp. 793-811.

3. The 1940's—War, Peace, and Education

A Decennial Vignette

THE INFERNO OF WAR, the search for peace, demobilization, postwar economic and social readjustment, rising inflation, and a resurgence of higher education with the return of the veterans were prominent national themes in the 1940's. The first academic year of the new decade, 1940-41, saw a country divided over the issues of neutrality, aid to presumable allies, and potential participation in World War II. With the Japanese attack upon Pearl Harbor, Dec. 7, 1941, the American people closed ranks and, in remarkable unanimity, devoted their resources, leadership, and manpower to their share of waging and winning the war against Nazi Germany, Fascist Italy, and Imperial Japan. By 1945, about 12,000,000 men and women were in the armed services, and some 260,000 lives had been lost. The cost of the war in life and money was incredible, but economically it restored a seeming prosperity.

Pursuant to an over-rapid demobilization, millions of service persons suddenly were returned home. Their reabsorption into, and readjustment to, civilian life caused some social and economic dislocation, but generally the transition was quicker and more successful than had seemed possible. The pent-up consumer demand, foreign aid requirements, the economic and military needs soon to arise in relation to the Korean war, and the continued education of many veterans facilitated the nation's economic recovery after World War II.

The search for peace through the United Nations and other channels was only partially successful, and, henceforth, the mushroom shadow of atomic warfare over all people was a reality of life as the outlines of the "cold war" with the communist powers emerged in the late 1940's. On the social and economic front, the effects of the war and postwar national policies produced a continually mounting national debt, further restrictions on business and industry, increased labor union activity, more social welfare legislation, and more agricultural subsidies. Despite apparent economic growth in this decade, rising levels of prices, wages, and production costs fueled the engines of inflation. There was concern over the rise of allegedly communist-inspired groups, the rumblings of rebellious young people that seem mild in comparison to the protest movements of the 1960's, and alleged or actual instances of discrimination.[12] The interplaying forces of the war itself, demobilization, and recovery all contributed to a reassessment on the part of many citizens of national premises and priorities. The resultant pressures were contained effectively in the 1940's, but perhaps comprised the time fuse of the protest bomb that was set for a violent explosion in the 1960's.

Music and the arts, in patriotic patterns and pursuits, largely were in the nation's service in this decade, especially in the war years. The rise of television after the war signaled partial eclipse and radical format readjustment in radio and the movies. The mechanics of the mass media, that later were to become such potent instruments for bringing Americans face to face with themselves, their role in the nation and the world, and the horrors of war, were being developed in the 1940's and early 1950's. The seeing of themselves as others saw them, or in some facsimile thereof, was a revealing and often shocking experience to many citizens. What was the impact of this time of international violence, domestic turbulence, and troubled peace upon higher education in terms of students and institutions?

---

[12] Langsam, *World History Since 1870, op. cit.*, pp. 470-473.

Impact of the War Years on Enrollments

The prime emphases in the Walters articles throughout the 1940's were the effects of incipient war conditions, the war itself, and postwar developments upon higher education as they related to students and institutions. In 1940-41, despite a growing awareness of the consequences of the war abroad and anticipated military Selective Service obligations, there were increases in full-time and grand total enrollments of less than one per cent. The continuation of NYA support for about 10% of the full-time students and the provision of the 1940 Selective Training and Service Act that allowed drafted students to complete the 1940-41 academic year before induction help to explain the holding of collegiate enrollments at a near-standstill level. There were 883,594 full-time and 1,347,146 grand total students in 652 approved colleges and universities, exclusive of some teachers colleges and separate junior colleges. There was a drop of two per cent in the 243,141 freshmen in five large fields of study at 643 institutions. This decline reflected birthrate figures, as well as the early effects of the coming war upon the plans of young men. Dr. Walters' sense of the future was evident in the observation that "other factors, such as economic changes due to the war or changes in educational philosophy, may prevent population trends from having their normal effect on collegiate attendance."[13] Efforts already were being made at the national level to locate pure and applied science research experts in the colleges and universities who might be available to the government for national defense service. Many of the 90,000 faculty members reported for the institutions in the Walters surveys were engaged in defense projects, and the author asserted that all faculty members so contributed in the sense that education was a vital aspect of national preparedness. Contrary to the trend of the 1960's, when some schools considered dropping their ROTC programs, many institutions in 1940 were asking the Federal government for ROTC units. Because officers were needed in active service, most requests could not be approved. There were then 115 ROTC institutions in the country.[14]

By 1941-42, declines of 9.2% in full-time and 8.9% in grand total students were reported for 669 accredited institutions. These were

---

[13] Raymond Walters, "Statistics of Registration in American Universities and Colleges, 1940," *School & Society*, 52:1335, Dec. 14, 1940, pp. 601-619.
[14] *Ibid.*, pp. 609-610.

the first sharp enrollment drops since the depression years of 1932 and 1933, and were attributed to the effects of the Selective Service Act, as well as to the lure of high-paying defense jobs. At the freshman level, where the entrants were under draft age, the decline was only 4.5%. Generally, enrollments rose or held their own in areas where deferments were granted, such as engineering, medicine, dentistry, some sciences, and nursing. The losses were severe, and remained so throughout the war, in graduate arts and sciences programs, law schools, and teacher training.[15]

That the exodus from academic campus to armed camp was underway in 1942-43 is shown by the further drop of 9.5% in full-time and 13.9% in grand total students. At the same time, freshmen were down only 1.7%, reflective of their below-draft age and their response to advice from the War and Navy Departments that their continued education would be valuable in later military service. Evening college enrollments showed a loss of 30.8%, attributed to overtime work obligations of part-time students, armed services calls, tuition-free Federal courses, and gasoline rationing. Particular attention was called to an alarming loss of 22.7% in teacher training programs and the future danger of a grave teacher shortage, a refrain that was to reappear many times in later reports.[16]

In 1943-44, there were 458,713 full-time civilians and about 363,-000 military students in Army and Navy training units reported by 674 schools. The grand total enrollment was 745,297, and the tallied freshmen numbered 140,849. These counts kept the enrollment levels close to those of 1942-43, but the civilian full-time student group suffered a near-40% loss and the civilian grand total was down some 30%. The statistics for that year were somewhat flexible because of the rapid ingress and egress of military trainees, but it was only their presence that precluded financial crises in hundreds of institutions. Schools without military units were hard-hit in finances and students, but managed to survive. It was not intended that the more than 400 schools holding military training contracts would make a profit, but such operations did permit those institutions to keep their faculties occupied and physical plants operating in educational service impor-

---

[15] Raymond Walters, "Statistics of Attendance in American Universities and Colleges, 1941," *School & Society*, 54:1407, Dec. 3, 1941, pp. 539-559.

[16] Raymond Walters, "Statistics of Attendance in American Universities and Colleges, 1952," *School & Society*, 56:1983, Dec. 20, 1952, pp. 391-402.

tant to the nation. Understandably, an outstanding feature of collegiate attendance that year was the enrollment of women. In the five freshman fields reported, there were 92,240 women, for an increase of seven per cent, and a decline in men enrollees of 62.7%. With the sons gone to war, many families now concentrated on the education of daughters, and the young women eagerly grasped the opportunity afforded them. They studied the arts and sciences particularly, and did much to keep the torch of liberal education burning in the dark war years.[17]

The nadir of wartime enrollments was reached in 1944-45, with totals of 608,750 full-time and 925,084 grand total students in 679 approved schools; these totals were nearly one-third below the rolls of 1939-40. In some institutions, men registrants had fallen by 50-94% in the five war years. The financial shoe continued to pinch, especially for the institutions that did not have military service units. In 1944, even the schools with such units began to suffer, because of the departure of their military trainees for active service in large numbers. The bind was especially tight upon the private schools, where tuition normally provided 50% of their income. Staff curtailments, use of endowment funds, special gifts, and absence leaves for faculty members on duty assignments in the armed forces, government, and industry were devices relied upon to stave off financial disaster. Even the state universities were restricted by legislative appropriations reflecting lower enrollments. Only the women's colleges seemed to escape dire financial problems as the enrollments of women reached new highs in 1944. There was much concern about the financial future of all institutions, and already the enrollment of an estimated 650-700,000 veterans at the end of the war was being anticipated. Also, over 600,000 military personnel were taking correspondence courses offered by USAFI [United States Armed Forces Institute] and some 85 colleges and universities.[18]

With 671,857 full-time and 985,227 grand total students in 645 reporting schools, enrollments began to rise sharply in 1945-46, but still were nearly 22% below 1939, the last peacetime year. Some 90,000 veterans in the above totals were taking courses under Public

[17] Raymond Walters, "Statistics of Attendance in American Universities and Colleges, 1943," *School & Society*, 58:1153, Dec. 25, 1943, pp. 484-494; and Raymond Walters, "Analysis of 1943 Attendance, 30 Representative Universities," *School & Society*, 59:1520, Feb. 12, 1944, pp. 100-107.

[18] Raymond Walters, "Statistics of Attendance in American Universities and Colleges, 1944," *School & Society*, 60:1565, Dec. 23, 1944, pp. 402-412.

Laws 346 and 16 that covered tuition and, for full-time study, subsistence allowances at the institutions they chose. Those students, 80,000 of whom were full-time, largely accounted for an increase of some 16% in full-time enrollment over 1944. By and large, the veterans in this and later years elected studies in technological, business, preprofessional, and professional areas; relatively few chose the arts and sciences and education programs. Since the war in Europe only ended on May 8, 1945 (V-E Day), and the victory over Japan was not official until August 14, 1945 (V-J Day), it had been impossible for veterans in large numbers to be ready for collegiate enrollment before Oct. 1, 1945, by which date most institutions were in session. The fact that they were being transported home in late 1945 at the rate of 600,000 a month indicated, however, that enrollments would be booming in the months ahead.[19]

The Postwar Years and the Veterans

All hands acknowledged that a new era began in 1946-47, when the nation embarked in earnest upon the collegiate training of the millions of qualified military service veterans. There were over 2,000,-000 students in 1,749 colleges and universities that year, and about half of them were veterans. In the 668 approved institutions reporting to Dr. Walters, there were 1,331,138 full-time students, including 714,477 veterans, and a grand total of 1,718,862—both were record totals. The full-time figure was some 57% above the 1939 prewar peacetime count. Veterans were a significant enrollment component in various school categories as follows: 131 universities and large institutions of complex organization, 57%; 557 independent four-year colleges of arts and sciences, 44%; 287 independent technical schools or institutes, 61%; 201 independent teachers colleges and normal schools, 41%; and 650 junior colleges, 43%. In this and later years, the veterans, by and large, were serious students, who performed at least as well as, and usually better than, their non-veteran counterparts. In general, they ignored those extracurricular activities that, in reflection of their maturity and experience, they deemed frivolous.[20] Many were married and had children, and housing was

---

19 Raymond Walters, "Statistics of Attendance in American Universities and Colleges, 1945," *School & Society*, 62:1618, Dec. 29, 1945, pp. 412-419.

20 Raymond Walters, "Statistics of Attendance in American Universities and Colleges, 1946," *School & Society*, 64:1669, Dec. 21, 1946, pp. 428-438.

a problem for them and their institutions. Often they were quartered in former military barracks that were moved quickly to the college campuses and frequently referred to as "vet villages." On many campuses, it was 10 to 15 years before these "temporary" housing facilities could be replaced by permanent residence halls.

The high tide of veteran enrollments came in 1947-48, when 1,149,933 veterans were included in the grand total of 2,338,226 students in over 1,750 institutions as reported by the U.S. Office of Education. The 716 schools covered in the Walters survey reported 1,556,559 full-time students and a grand total of 2,178,257. In the schools with comparable data, this meant increases of 9.7% in full-time and 18.8% in part-time students over 1946-47. Significantly, the freshman figures reported comparably revealed a 23% drop in men and a 3.7% decline of freshman women. The veteran bulge was still in the educational pipeline, but a few years hence there would come enrollment declines. Reasons for a veteran fall-off in freshmen, and later in the upper classes, were that many of them were taking jobs, some had family obligations, and a large number pursued the many accelerated programs provided by colleges for their benefit.[21]

Enrollments in 1948-49 showed an increase of less than one per cent in full-time attendance and a 4.5% increase in part-time figures, but this was the peak year for the decade in collegiate numbers. In 726 schools in the *School & Society* survey, there were 1,580,783 full-time and 1,931,979 grand total students. In all 1,800 institutions in the land, the U.S. Office of Education indicated that there were about 2,410,000 students, or 3.1% more than in the previous year. Freshmen in the areas reported, however, showed a 10% decline. This largely reflected the low birthrate of the depression years, but even then Dr. Walters and others were pointing to the mid-1950's, when the high schools would be flooded by students born after World War II. Soon thereafter, they would be ready for college. The need for financial, physical, and faculty resources in the next decade were being anticipated. The veteran enrollment in all schools was down to 953,247, about 42% of total collegiate counts and a 17% decrease over 1947-48. In 674 comparable approved institutions,

---

[21] Raymond Walters, "Statistics of Attendance in American Universities and Colleges, 1947," *School & Society*, 66:1722, Dec. 27, 1947, pp. 488-498; Raymond Walters, "Statistics of Attendance in American Universities and Colleges, 1948," *School & Society*, 68:1773, Dec. 18, 1948, pp. 419-430.

there were 686,368 full-time veterans, a decrease of 11%.[22] Collegiate administrators and faculties who manned the academic ramparts in the crowded years of the postwar 1940's deserved the nation's gratitude. To accommodate numbers that were three-fourths larger than the prewar 1939 peak, they used classrooms, laboratories, and housing facilities to the utmost of their efficiency, and faculties carried heavy loads and taught unusually large classes. It was an exercise in appreciation of, and tribute to, the millions of GI's for service to their country and for the high quality of their academic work.[23]

In the last year of the decade, 1949-50, enrollments for 713 comparably reporting schools showed a decline of 3.7% in full-time and a 1.1% increase in grand total students. In all 753 reporting universities and four-year colleges, there were 1,567,500 full-time students, 427,295 part-time students, and 1,994,795 in all. Almost 38% still were veterans among the full-time students. The U.S. Office of Education, in some 1,850 institutions, tabulated 2,659,021 students, in comparison to 2,408,249 for the previous year. For schools in this group reporting comparably both years, the increase was a bare 0.1%. This final report of the 1940's also was the 30th annual survey prepared by Dr. Walters in the *School & Society* series.[24]

---

[22] *Ibid.*

[23] *Loc. cit.*

[24] Raymond Walters, "Statistics of Attendance in American Universities and Colleges, 1949," *School & Society,* 70:1826, Dec. 17,1949, pp. 388-398.

4. Security and Seeds of Disorder in the 1950's

The National Setting

As IN PREVIOUS DECADES, collegiate enrollments in the 1950's reflected the facts and fictions of American life at home and abroad, and, increasingly, they came to have their own impact upon the course of national events. The late 1940's were marked by a "cold war" waged on all but the fighting fronts, as the U.S.S.R. sought to expand the communist sphere of control and the U.S. strove to contain it. The new decade dawned with a flareup of "hot" war in the Far East. In June, 1950, after the invasion of South Korea by North Korean troops, the U.S., in association with 15 other nations under UN sponsorship, undertook to repel this new aggression. The struggle levied a heavy toll in terms of manpower, resources, and disillusionment with the search for peace.

In the second administration of Democratic Pres. Harry S. Truman, 1949-53, there was much concern over the Korean conflict, the "cold war" with Russia, and the communist threat at home, but there was no intensive legislative activity on the domestic front. There were incidents of corruption in high places in the government, some serious spying episodes that accounted for leaks of classified information to communist agents, and much noise was made by procommunist sympathizers. Legislation aiming at the control of such activity was enacted. By 1953, the degree of the Federal government's control over the social and economic life of its citizens was significant.

World War II General of the Army Dwight David Eisenhower, a Republican, served as President of the U.S. in the 1953-61 years. In 1953, he was successful in negotiating a Korean armistice. His administrations were marked by a conservative thrust, as efforts were made to slow up the welfare-state trend, balance the budget, and exercise economy in government. Even so, the nation still moved, even if more slowly, along the liberal road first charted by the Roosevelt administrations in the depression 1930's. The censure of Sen. Joseph R. McCarthy (R., Wis.) in 1954, for what many regarded as overzealous efforts in the field of anti-communism, was an event of much interest, especially on college campuses.

An epochal Supreme Court decision in 1954 held that segregation in state schools was a "denial of the equal protection of the laws." This decision launched the civil rights movement that aimed at progress in integration affecting education, transportation, housing, labor, entertainment, and sports. In pursuance of that decision, and despite some violence, significant integration progress was made in the above-mentioned fields. Aside from a recession in 1958, the Eisenhower administrations were marked by prosperity at home, effective representation of American interests abroad, and a deceleration of welfare-statism.[25] In some respects, they allowed time for consolidation and stock-taking after three decades of dynamic change. The early years of the decade, at least, were marked by a tendency to conformity in social life, the search for security, the flight to suburbia by middle-class whites aspiring to affluence, and a filling-up of the inner city by disadvantaged ethnic minorities, especially the blacks. The violent seeds of the 1960's still were being planted in the flaccid 1950's.

In 1957, the Space Age was entered when the Russians launched Sputnik I, the first orbiting satellite. By 1959, both the Russians and the Americans had placed men in orbit. The Soviet lead in space technology gave rise to great criticism of American education. It was

---

[25] Langsam, *World History Since 1870, op. cit.,* pp. 470-475.

often unjustified, but it caused much constructive attention to be given to needed educational reform.

Parallel Patterns in Higher Education

Reflections on the 1950's reveal certain patterns in higher education emphases and enrollments that merit summary attention. The receding haze of World War II in the first years of the decade soon was obscured by the smoke and fire of the limited, but hot, conflict in Korea. The shadow of this conflagration hung over college campuses and collegians in the early and mid-1950's and affected enrollments, first as a depressant and later as a stimulant. The trend in numbers was downward through 1952-53, but, thereafter, a rise began that culminated in the enrollment explosion of the 1960's. Financial problems for institutions and students were items of concern throughout the decade. Private and municipal institutions, especially, felt the effects of escalating costs and sought new sources of funds. State-supported institutions petitioned legislatures for increased aid, and began to seek additional assistance from private sectors. Tuition fees rose, and students felt the pinch financially. Increasing attention was given to the need for more student financial aid in the form of scholarships, loans, grants, and part-time work. Government and industry moved to supplement the resources of the schools in this vital area. Financial aid officers came into their own on college campuses as a virtually new profession.

Students in the early and mid-1950's generally were not activists. For various reasons, including military service, many were older and more mature than the usual collegians. World War II, the "cold war," and the Korean conflict were sobering experiences. There was a concern for security, personal as well as social, and millions of Americans, especially the whites, sought a profitable and comfortable place for themselves and their families in an increasingly affluent society. Students were serious, but showed no great propensity for "involvement." Many professors complained of their seeming apathy about nonacademic concerns, and they subsequently have been referred to as the "quiet" or the "silent" generation.

Superior Students and Testing

The decade of the 1950's also was a time of much discussion about "selective admissions" and "qualifications" for the college-bound. As numbers mounted in later years, many private, and some public, institutions limited enrollments and raised admissions standards. State legislatures and public universities began to be mindful of restricting their out-of-state students.

A negative view was taken by professors and colleges of remedial work for ill-prepared high school graduates. The argument was that such tutorial or make-up work was not the function of the colleges. On the other hand, there was much interest in the so-called superior student, and academic doors swung open wide for him in terms of admission, financial aid, and programs for the talented. Careful consideration was given to the acceleration and enrichment of academic programs for able students. Most illustrative and highly successful was the Advanced Placement Program pioneered by the College Entrance Examination Board. This program comprehended college-level courses in high school, national examinations for the participants, and the granting of placement and credit in college courses in recognition of the advanced work of these superior students. The emphasis upon screening for college-level ability placed increased priority upon college aptitude tests. The CEEB Scholastic Aptitude Test (SAT) long had dominated the admissions testing scene in the Eastern schools, and it began to assume greater prominence in other sectors of the land. With increasing numbers and needs for tests in admissions and counseling, another testing service arose to compete with the CEEB and share in servicing the nation's schools, their graduates, and the colleges. This was the American College Testing Program (ACT), founded in Iowa City, Iowa, in 1959, that, by the close of the decade, was making its service available across the nation.

The Student and the Machine

This decade also ushered in the time when electronic data processing based on the ubiquitous IBM or other cards became the record symbol of higher education. Unquestionably, machines became indispensable in the handling of the massive data collections that now are so important in the higher education system. On the one hand, they made identification of individual students possible and made available a host of services that otherwise would have been impossible. On the other hand, they gave rise to an alleged impersonalization, whereby the student's identity was more digital than individual. It is ironic to note the collegiate protest against machine records along-side the willingness of students and the general population to accept the same principles of record-keeping on their gasoline and department store credit cards, not to mention the social security system. This writer asserts that the furor over IBM cards merely reflects the rising crescendo of protest against student depersonalization generally in higher education in the 1950's and 1960's. Against this background of national events and developments in higher education, a review of registrations in the 1950's may be more meaningful.

Enrollment Records in the 1950's

In 1950-51, the decline that had begun the previous year continued, with 1,414,428 full-time, 433,759 part-time, and 1,848,187 grand total students enrolled in 770 reporting institutions. In comparable situations, this reflected a drop of 9.4% in full-time students and a decrease of 7.1% in the grand total. These decreases reflected the graduation the previous June of record-breaking senior classes, made up primarily of veterans, and the fall-off in freshman enrollees. The veteran enrollment itself in 1950-51 was 554,614, nearly one-third less than the number enrolled in 1949. Another factor was the sharp freshman decline of 11.8% in full-time male students, and even a loss of 2.3% in freshman women. Primarily, this reflected the low birthrate in the early 1930's.[26]

The next year, 1951-52, brought further declines in the comparable schools of 11.4% in full-time and 7.8% in grand total students. Part-time students were up by 4.6%, but the freshmen reached their low point in the 1950's, with a loss of another 6.4%. The impact of the new Selective Service regulations and the Korean conflict had not been heavy yet at the college level, since full-time college men in good standing generally were subject to deferment. Over 300,000 students under the so-called World War II GI Bill of Rights still were in school. There was much concern over the freshman decrease, especially in education programs where low salaries for teachers appeared to be a barrier for entering students. The part-time enrollment increase reflected promotional programs by colleges, increasing tuition-support policies by industry, and the tendency

---

[26] Raymond Walters, "Statistics of Attendance in American Universities and Colleges, 1950," *School & Society*, 72:1879, Dec. 23, 1950, pp. 401-413.

among some students with family obligations to complete their degree programs at night on a part-time basis.[27]

The low level of enrollments in the 1950's came in 1952-53, when 830 institutions reported 1,293,524 full-time, 462,848 part-time, and 1,756,372 grand total enrollees. In comparable data situations, the percentage decreases in the full-time, part-time, and grand total categories, respectively, were 1.5%, 2.8%, and 1.8%. The striking feature of 1952-53 enrollments was the freshman increase of 11.5% for men and 8.1% for women in the categories surveyed. The entering students that year still derived from a low birthrate year; thus, other factors had to explain the rise. Much publicity recently had been given to the nation's need for, and the opportunities in, "engineering, science, business, agriculture, school teaching, nursing, and other fields." Another potent factor, in view of the Korean involvement, was the draft deferment permitted by Selective Service.[28]

After slight increases in 1953-54, enrollment gains continued in 1954-55, with comparable reports showing increases of 6.8%, 9.7%, and 7.6%, respectively, in full-time, part-time, and grand total categories. The actual counts in 846 reporting schools were 1,383,750 full-time students and 1,895,280 in the grand total. Freshmen in the reported groups were up again by 9.2%, with significant gains of 19.4% in education and nine per cent in engineering.[29]

Dr. Walters retired as president of the University of Cincinnati in 1955, but continued his responsibility for the *School & Society* collegiate enrollment reports through 1959-60. The 1955-56 study was the first written in his president emeritus status. In 886 approved schools, there were reported 1,612,225 full-time students and a grand total of 2,111,485. In comparably reporting institutions, there were increases of nine per cent in full-time students, 6.5% in part-time registrants, and 8.3% in the grand total. Freshmen showed an increase of 9.4% over 1954-55. The professional and technical areas of study showed the biggest percentage gain in new students, but, as for several decades, the actual numbers were largest in the arts and

---

[27] Raymond Walters, "Statistics of Attendance in American Universities and Colleges, 1951," *School & Society*, 74:1931, Dec. 22, 1951, pp. 385-398.

[28] Raymond Walters, "Statistics of Attendance in American Universities and Colleges, 1953," *School & Society*, 78:2021, Dec. 12, 1953, pp. 177-188.

[29] Raymond Walters, "Statistics of Attendance in American Universities and Colleges, 1954," *School & Society*, 80:2048, Dec. 11, 1954, pp. 177-188.

sciences. That the freshmen in 1955-56 came out of high school classes smaller than those in 1939-40—6,478,431 as compared to 7,059,-000 according to the U.S. Office of Education report—testified to the rising percentage of college-age attendance. Engineering enrollments experienced their first significant rise since 1946, bolstered by the large sophomore and freshman classes then in school. Much emphasis in the middle 1950's, in reflection of the dawning Space Age needs and technical rivalry with the U.S.S.R., was placed upon the need for students in engineering and the sciences.[30]

By 1956-57, U.S. collegiate enrollments exceeded the previous peaks of 1947 and 1948, the years of the veteran bulge. In 901 accredited institutions, there were 1,724,897 full-time students, 559,-222 part-time enrollees, and a grand total of 2,284,119. The respective percentage increases were 6.5%, 11.5%, and 7.8%. Veterans numbered 709,147, of whom 408,760 were from the Korean conflict. This was the high mark for veteran enrollments in the post-Korean years. The freshman gain of 3.3% over 1955-56 in the reported categories indicated that about 40% of high school graduates were entering college that year.[31]

By 1957-58, the survey included 930 accredited universities, four-year colleges, and technical schools—representing well over 1,000 separate campuses—and comprehended 1,755,103 full-time students, a grand total of 2,415,214, and 406,883 freshmen in five fields. The trend was still up, with gains of 2.7% in full-time, eight per cent in part-time, 4.2% in grand total, and 0.3% in freshman students. There were 400,000 more full-time students than the accredited schools had attracted five years previously, in 1952-53. The author, emphasizing that these students derived from low birthrate years, pointed out that here was "a portent of what is to happen when, in a few years, campus gates will be besieged by pupils now in the primary grades who represent the pronounced rise in the birth rate which followed World War II and still continues." The provision of physical facilities and faculty personnel were obvious problems that resulted in freshman limitations in many private institutions. The effect was to spread enrollments over more institutions in the nation, but even some state and municipal schools were restricting admission

---

[30] Raymond Walters, "Statistics of Attendance in American Universities and Colleges, 1955," *School & Society*, 82:2074, Dec. 10, 1955, pp. 178-189.
[31] Raymond Walters, "Statistics of Attendance in American Universities and Colleges, 1956," *School & Society*, 84:2100, Dec. 8, 1956, pp. 191-202.

of nonresidents.[32] In the same year, the U.S. Office of Education, for the first time, reported an excess of 3,000,000 students in about 1,850 institutions.[33]

In 1958-59, 944 institutions covered in the survey reported 1,828,-660 full-time and 2,531,755 grand total students, increases of 4.1% and 5.4%, respectively; part-time enrollees were up 8.6%. These larger enrollments had not been expected, since scholarship entitlements for 55,000 Korean veterans had expired, there was an economic recession in 1958, and another large class had been graduated in June, 1958. The prime reason for the continuation of the enrollment lift was the 7.1% rise in freshmen reported in the surveyed areas, for a total of 445,870. Increases of freshmen were noted in education programs, arts and sciences, business administration, and agriculture, but engineering had a 7.6% decrease. Again, the author reminded his readers of the high birthrates of the 1940's and the implications they had for high enrollments in the early 1960's in respect to facilities and faculties.[34]

The 40th and final report prepared by Dr. Walters, in 1959-60, revealed modest increases that pushed enrollments to an all-time high for that time. In 995 reporting and accredited institutions, there were 1,973,948 full-time students and a grand total of 2,811,704. In comparable situations, these totals reflected respective increases of four per cent and 3.6%, and the freshman increase was 4.5%. In 1,952 institutions, the U.S. Office of Education also counted a record total of 3,402,297 students. In his last report, the author expressed great concern over the problems of training adequate teaching staffs for the schools and colleges. Also, he lamented the percentage decline of students entering engineering programs that had begun in 1958-59, but was pleased with the upturn of the numbers taking science and mathematics majors—a factor no doubt related to the space race between the U.S and the U.S.S.R. Subsequent to the publication of the 40th report, Dr. Walters' last contribution was his review of *Four Decades of U.S. Collegiate Enrollments,* issued in 1960, and for

---

[32] Raymond Walters, "Statistics of Attendance in American Universities and Colleges, 1957," *School & Society*, 85:2121, Dec. 7, 1957, pp. 371-386.

[33] U.S. Office of Education, *Digest of Educational Statistics, 1968, op. cit.,* p. 68.

[34] Raymond Walters, "Statistics of Attendance in American Universities and Colleges, 1958," *School & Society*, 86:2142, Dec. 6, 1958, pp. 427-440.

which this writer has been most grateful as a reference in the preparation of this book.[35]

[35] Raymond Walters, "Statistics of Attendance in American Universities and Colleges, 1959-60," *School & Society*, 88:2165, Jan. 2, 1960, pp. 5-20; Raymond Walters, *Four Decades of U.S. Collegiate Enrollments* (New York: Society for the Advancement of Education, 1960), pp. 1-24. See, also, *School & Society*, 88:2169; Feb. 27, 1960, pp. 85-92. This writer has tried not to be needlessly repetitive of narrative, facts, and tables included in this document, but he does refer readers to it for valuable information.

5. The Violent Decade—
Challenge and Change in
the 1960's

The Kennedy Era

SOME PERSPECTIVE on the flow of events—both foreign and domestic—is essential to an understanding of higher education happenings in the 1960's. Few prophets in 1959 foresaw the extent of challenge and change to come in the new decade. After a closely contested campaign in 1960, John F. Kennedy, a Democrat, was elected President. His personal charisma and liberal legislative program, labeled the "New Frontier," aroused strong support from a wide cross section of the population, especially the young people. His youth, vitality, capacity to inspire, and his clamant inaugural call for Americans to "ask not what your country can do for you," but ". . . what you can do for your country," gave credence to the assertion that ". . . the torch has been passed to a new generation of Americans. . . ." The formation of the Peace Corps and the ready response to it seemed to signalize a special commitment to social service in the youth of the early 1960's. The President's interest in, and concern for, music, the arts, and scholarship gave a unique intellectual thrust to our national leadership in his administration. Numerous academicians found themselves in the seats of the mighty. An attractive wife and young children added much familial appeal, and many Americans joined with John F. Kennedy in his sentimental assertion that this was "Camelot."

The elation of the nation was great when Lt. Col. John Glenn orbited the earth three times in 1962 on an epochal space flight. In domestic affairs, Federal support of education was expanded, and aid was extended to depressed areas. Despite favorable legislation, however, civil rights activism continued, culminating, in 1963, with a "Freedom March" on Washington. There was trouble with inflation, and the President insisted upon a roll-back of steel prices that did not endear him to the captains of industry.

Meanwhile, relations worsened with Cuba and Russia. The President absorbed the onus of the ill-fated Bay of Pigs invasion in Cuba, but, in a dramatic and tense "eyeball-to-eyeball" confrontation, in which he was the U.S. protagonist, the U.S.S.R. agreed to remove its missiles from its island protégé in the Caribbean. In the same years, a war cloud that later was to envelop much of Southeast Asia was taking shape over South Vietnam. U.S. aid to encourage economic and political progress there had been granted since the mid-1950's, but, in 1959, the Viet Cong and the North Vietnamese undertook to overthrow the South Vietnamese government. U.S. troops, in the capacity of advisers, were sent to South Vietnam; by 1963, these troops numbered 16,300.

The tragedy that so often has trailed the Kennedy family intervened to cut short the saga of the "New Frontier" and, in a sense, the new generation. On Nov. 22, 1963, in Dallas, Tex., John F. Kennedy was mortally wounded by an assassin's bullets, fired by a sharpshooter from, of all places, a textbook warehouse. The political edifice of such seeming promise to so many came crashing to the ground with an impact that still was reverberating at the close of the decade.

The Season of the "Great Society" and Lyndon Johnson

Their personalities as well as their political programs gave a special distinction to our national leaders in the 1960's. Lyndon B.

Johnson, the "tall Texan" who had risen from a schoolteaching assignment to the Vice Presidency of the nation, was sworn in as President of the U.S. on that dark day of the assassination in Dallas. With great dynamism, enormous drive, and broad perspective, he led the nation on its search for the "Great Society." History well may credit his administration with the most extensive program of significant legislation on record in a comparable period, certainly since the "New Deal" period.

The "Great Society" program included the enactment of the Civil Rights Act of 1964, one of the significant milestones in civil rights history. The Medicare program and increased Social Security benefits appealed to the aged, and an updating of the immigration statutes eased restrictions on newcomers to the country. Developing crisis conditions in the cities brought the creation of a Department of Housing and Urban Development with Cabinet status. There was the beginning of a "war on poverty," in which special attention was given to the needs of the poor and "culturally disadvantaged." Community action groups were sponsored to bring aid programs directly to the people, and the poor themselves were recruited as advisers and even administrators in many such Federally supported projects. Integration was pushed vigorously not only in housing and schools, but also in business, industry, labor, and the technical trades. The first massive Federal aid to schools came in the Elementary and Secondary Education Act of 1965. Attention given to the special problems of the disadvantaged in learning was reflected in Project Head Start for preschool children, Upward Bound for secondary level pupils, and other talent search efforts to locate and motivate students with potential promise who otherwise might not have an opportunity to enter college or take other advanced training. Higher education also shared in the largesse of Federal funds to an unprecedented degree.

Along with apparent progress in the social and educational areas, problems arose in respect to race, youth, the economy, and foreign relations. In the long run, the Achilles heel of the Johnson administration proved to be the war in Vietnam. As pressure by the Viet Cong and the North Vietnamese upon South Vietnam increased, American troops forsook an advisory status for an actual combat role. American involvement escalated rapidly in 1963, and, on the basis of the Gulf of Tonkin Resolution by Congress in 1964, the President authorized the bombing of North Vietnam and the sending of many thousands of additional troops to South Vietnam. The number rose from 23,300 "advisers" in 1964 to 542,500 combatants by Jan. 20, 1969. By the close of the decade, some 40,000 American fighting men had given their lives in this strange war.

At home, there was increasing strife involving civil rights, despite strong administrative leadership and significant legislative action in this area. "Sit-ins," "lay-ins," "teach-ins," "love-ins," "freedom marches," passive resistance, civil disobedience, and, finally, violence and rioting were the techniques of protest in the Johnsonian 1960's. Tragedy struck and racked the nation again in 1968, when Dr. Martin Luther King, Jr., the disciple of passive resistance, and Robert F. Kennedy, the heir apparent to the political mantle of his deceased brother, were felled by assassins.

On the economic side, the Johnson policy was one that called for providing both "guns and butter." It was decreed that the nation could afford to wage war in Vietnam and implement "Great Society" programs at the same time. As a matter of fact, the country displayed an enormous productive capacity with the gross national product reaching $932,300,000,000 by 1969. In 1960, the Federal budget was $75,500,000,000, and was climbing toward $200,000,000,-000 by the end of the decade. In the same period, the national debt rose from $286,500,000,000 to $371,400,000,000. Contrary to this escalation in production and expenditures, the dollar declined some 25% in value in the decade. Inflation, by 1969, was rising by about six per cent per year, exacting a heavy national toll in the 1960's for the prosperity that it accompanied.

With the Beatles group from England setting the tone in the early 1960's, a new style of music emerged that had high appeal for the young and was heard in wonderment by the old. Long hair, unconventional clothes, a peculiar patois, alienation from parents, protestations of love, the use of the flower as a symbol, and a seeming wish to resign from society were some earmarks of a new "hippie" subculture that flourished among the youth in the later years of the decade. There was much emphasis on a generation gap that allegedly made communication difficult between those over and under age 30. A relaxation of many sexual inhibitions, the rise of obscenity under the guise of free speech, and the widespread use of the contraceptive pill all were evidence of changing social mores. Drug abuse by adolescents and college-age youth became widespread. The stage, the movie theater, and a segment of the press exhibited forms of entertainment and other programs that were unprecedented in the freedom of their presentation; there was little left that could be negated on grounds of obscenity. In dress, the era was one of extremes. Some men wore beads; many women donned trousers. The mini-skirt was the badge of the coed, but, in 1969, she often concealed it under a maxi-coat. Hairstyles ranged from the crew-cut of the early 1960's to the Samson-like locks of the hippies and the "natural" Afro-cuts of the blacks in 1969. Accompanying these developments was the rise of the peace movement in opposition to the Vietnam war and the military draft. Peace marches, protest meetings, boycotts, and anti-war moratoriums were features of American life in the 1960's.

Even in religion, the decade was one of iconoclasm. The evangelicals and fundamentalists took issue with the liberals and libertarians. There was an ecumenical thrust in the mid-1960's that attracted much support—and opposition—among traditional denominationalists in the Protestant groups. The winds of liberal change even swept inside the Roman Catholic Church doors in reflection of the view of Pope John XXIII that it was time to let in a bit of fresh air. Permission for masses to be conducted in vernacular languages was one aspect of reform, and more consultation with the clerical bodies developed.

By the end of the decade, however, a new Pope had reined in the liberals and reasserted the doctrine of papal infallibility, and the Protestant-oriented ecumenical movement had lost some of its power. After exposure to "God is dead" theologians for some years, many felt, by 1969, not only that God was alive, but there was a need for a moral reversion and a sincere search for Him.

From Johnson to Nixon

After an unusual honeymoon with Congress and the country that resulted in a spate of legislation in 1963-64, Lyndon B. Johnson ran for re-election in his own right in 1964. The result was an overwhelming victory over Republican Barry Goldwater, who posed a conservative option for the nation, as shown by the 586-52 electoral vote and 61% majority of the popular vote. In his second administration, however, Johnson's popularity and effective leadership declined in rough proportion to the degree of U.S. military commitment and seeming lack of success in Vietnam. There was much talk of a "credibility gap" in the relations between the administration and the press and people. In a surprise gesture, Pres. Johnson announced in 1968 that he would not seek election for another term. In the ensuing campaign, another very close contest saw the defeat of the Democrats under the leadership of Hubert H. Humphrey, Vice President under Johnson, and the victory of Richard M. Nixon and the Republicans.

Nixon had served as Vice President under Eisenhower, narrowly was defeated for the Presidency by Kennedy in 1960, and made one of the most remarkable comebacks in American political history to win in 1968. Nixon was a spokesman for what might be termed progressive conservatism. His aim was not to undo the progress of the past, but to slacken the hectic pace that had been pursued since 1960. The first few months of his administration served as a time for consolidation and stock-taking before the announcement of new policies. There was little legislative activity in the first year of the administration, but many of Nixon's proposals on Social Security, welfare, poverty, hunger, and environmental control suggested the continuation of progressive policies in most areas of social concern. There was indication of a willingness to slow down the impact of school integration in the South, but the tactic of delay was negated by a U.S. Supreme Court decision, and the Federal government then proceeded to enforce the law—the focus being on Mississippi schools. Crime prevention, revenue-sharing with the states, and anti-inflation measures were other domestic subjects of Nixon's attention. His nomination of a conservative-leaning South Carolinian as a Supreme Court justice was disapproved by the Senate, although not necessarily on ideological grounds.

The prime Nixon achievement in 1969 was a slowdown of the war in Vietnam. He began the withdrawal of American troops, emphasized the increasing Vietnamization of the war, and put other countries on notice that they must look less to the U.S. in the future and rely more on their own resources for their security. Before the year was out, a national lottery system for military draft purposes was implemented. Although the Moratorium March on Washington in November mobilized some 300,000 peaceful protesters against the Vietnam war, the effort was largely ineffective. The President ended his first year in office with evidence of strong support from the population segments that increasingly were becoming known as the "silent majority." Without question, the penultimate scientific achievement of the decade came on July 20, 1969, when two American astronauts, Neil A. Armstrong and Col. Edward E. Aldrin, Jr., became the first men to walk on the moon. This exciting event was the culmination of many years of intensive research, engineering, and exploration in space. The occasion was an emotional rallying point for nearly all Americans, and attracted the keen attention and respect of people and nations all over the world. It was a fitting testimony to the efficacy of American scientific and administrative capacity when applied to a physical objective. Such success and coordination, it was hoped, also would be successful if and when applied in like degree to domestic problems.

Impact of the Violent 1960's on Higher Education

Mushrooming enrollments ushered in the 1960's, and much consideration was given to the provision of the physical facilities, finance, and faculty needed to serve the rising millions. The growth in total enrollments from 1960 to 1969 in all institutions of higher education—from about 3,600,000 to an estimated 7,980,000—is a statistical measure of the challenge of the decade. In the main, institutions and the nation deserve high commendation for the herculean efforts expended to accommodate the massive numbers that enrolled in these crowded years. It was an educational achievement unparalleled in the history of this or any other nation.

As already suggested, the Federal government increasingly gave its financial support to higher education. This aid was reflected in the Higher Education Act of 1965 and the continuation of the National Defense Education Act of 1958 that undergirded an ever-rising level of loans and grants to needy students. Majors in the healing arts professions, teaching, and the sciences were notable beneficiaries of government support. Extensive state, local, and private scholarship and loan programs provided additional aid in significant sums.

With the rise of the civil rights movement, there developed an increasing interest in providing educational opportunity for the underprivileged or disadvantaged minority-group students, especially the blacks. There was mounting criticism of aptitude or entrance tests as vehicles for a disguised discrimination against blacks and other minority groups. It was alleged that their cultural backgrounds were not attuned to the abstractions, literary allusions, and concepts reflective of middle- and upper-class Americans that, according to the critics, were so salted into the national aptitude tests that they served as unjustifiable barriers to college entrance of minorities. National testing organizations moved to develop testing instruments that would more effectively identify talent, aptitude, and promise of success in college among disadvantaged groups. More and more, black leaders and students contended that it should be possible not only to enter, but to succeed in college without sacrificing the cultural base that spawned them. On the other hand, many argued that the cultural base from which any of us derive should be adaptable and subject to change as reason and common consent may suggest. In recoil from the testing "hang-up," to use a cliché of the "now" generation, demands arose for the removal of any "qualifications" for admission and there was a call for open admissions in public institutions in the later years of the 1960's. Where this was not feasible, and especially in the private schools, it was argued that a certain percentage of high-risk or academically marginal students should be admitted into normal baccalaurcate programs. Tutorial, intensive counseling, and generous financial aid programs were assumed to be necessary accoutrements of plans that identified and admitted these students. For the foreseeable future, the objective was to recruit from the minority groups a number of collegians roughly proportionate to their count in the population at large. That such recruitment and aid programs might be interpreted as reverse discrimination against sizable segments of the white population, especially in the middle and lower classes, was justified on the ground that the handicaps imposed by decades and centuries of discrimination against the minority groups should be overcome as soon as possible. Black students and faculty members assumed an increasingly active role in the recruitment of black applicants on many campuses. Enrollment data on a racial basis are sparse at best in the statistics of higher education; only in 1965 did the U.S. Office of Education begin to request racial data in its compliance surveys. In prior years, it was considered discriminatory to ask college students about their race, but, since then, the data base for significant studies has been created. Unquestionably, minority-group enrollments were far short of the percentages their numbers comprise in the total population, and there was much room for improvement on this score in the 1970's.

Another aspect of the racial pressure in higher education was the demand for Black Studies programs in dozens of institutions across the land. Curricula had to be revised, textbooks written, new studies undertaken, and teachers either trained or retrained for these courses. Crash programs in these areas were not always immediately successful, and many questions were raised about their academic authenticity. Even so, much good work was done and most educators concurred in the view that curricular redress in this area was long overdue. One important lesson that marginal students, whether from minority or majority groups, continually have to relearn is that there is no royal road to learning, no magic buttons, and no panaceas. Regrettably, the dropout rate still was excessive among marginal students and it was not always because of inability; too frequently it reflected lack of motivation, appropriate self-discipline, and encouragement from associates and peers. Academic attainment on any level less than a high-quality one will be self-defeating and disappointing. On the other hand, one of the bright lights of the 1960's was the commendable achievement of thousands of minority-group students who, in former years, would have been uninformed about, as well as financially unprepared and unmotivated for, college attendance. The leadership of these collegians trained in the 1960's will be of prime importance in the decade of the 1970's.

The multiplying millions of collegians in the 1960's gave a high priority to the services of faculty members. New faculty had to be recruited from age groups derived from low birthrate years, as a rule, and therefore enjoyed a buyer's position in the academic marketplace. From a professorial perspective, this was an unusual and advantageous situation. As a result, many reforms that long had been needed were achieved. Class teaching loads went down, more graduate teaching assistants aided the professors, there was more secretarial help, instructional materials were more plentiful, and salaries skyrocketed as institutions vied with each other to keep their academic posts manned. Unquestionably, many thousands of able and devoted faculty members deserved unlimited credit for sharing effectively in the education of so many millions of young Americans.

At the same time, there were faculty developments with implications that were not always fortunate. The twin service arm of collegiate teaching is research, and it received unprecedented emphasis in the decade of the 1960's. To a large degree, government-sponsored projects dominated the research scene in American colleges and universities. As problems pyramided both at home and abroad in the 1960's, the government and the nation increasingly relied upon the expertise in its institutions of higher education for investigations that would yield solutions. Indeed, it is not an overstatement to suggest that, if the changing answers to our continuing problems in American society and government are not found by collegiate researchers, often in teamwork with business, industry, and government, they may not be found at all. At any rate, financial subsidies in generous amounts supported the specific projects in which the Federal government had an immediate interest. National defense needs, as reflected in advanced weaponry, medical and health services, and the space sciences, were special areas of interest. As a result, the physical and biological sciences and the healing arts professions profited mightily from government sponsorship. The humanities and the social sciences were academic orphans in the government assistance field, and received aid that only could be regarded as lagniappe. It is clear that the needs of war, health, and space set the priorities in government support of higher education, but one wonders if solutions of the other great and as yet unsolved social problems of the 1960's would have been enhanced by greater aid for studies relating to them. The tendency was for government grants to be awarded to a minority of institutions, usually the 25-30 educational and research giants of the nation in both public and private areas. As some institutions have discovered, an over-dependence upon government-aided projects can create budgetary crises when cutbacks in Federal spending are announced. The academic world is a very prestige-conscious society, and the gaining of grants not only was important financially, but added status to the institutions and professors receiving them. Also, the rivalry for such subsidies gave rise to a technique of "grantsmanship" that often called for special or regular representatives on the Washington power scene to give effective representation to university interests. It was said, facetiously, that any good university had 10% of its faculty in the air at any one time on missions related to research or grants.

It is understandable that professors and their institutions took pride in their research and supporting grants. Hindsight suggests, however, that research in many institutions was overemphasized to the detriment of student interests. Given the stress on grants and research, reflected in salaries and promotions, too many professors elevated research and denigrated teaching in their scale of academic values. Students were thought of by some as necessary nuisances, but not ones that should take a lot of time nor require high-quality teaching. Many senior professors taught few classes, or none at all, and, whenever possible, junior faculty endeavored to follow their example. Students were herded into increasingly large classes on many campuses and often poorly taught by inexperienced graduate teaching assistants, who themselves often had to give higher priority to their research progress toward advanced degrees. Perhaps unconsciously, but assuredly, many faculties were inviting the student revolts so often lamented in the later 1960's. It took many violent reactions by students to bring good teaching back into more appropriate focus as an important university objective.

In response to pressing needs, as well as in pursuit of prestige, hundreds of institutions either launched into, or sought to upgrade, their programs of graduate and professional study. These programs were very expensive and inadequately supported in many instances. By the end of the 1960's, however, the annual output of the universities at the doctoral level was about 30,000, and Ph.D.'s in many areas had become "a glut on the market."[36] What to do with thousands of advanced degree holders who are highly trained in narrow specialties and may be unneeded could be one of the problems of the 1970's.

Professors in the 1960's also exerted a rising measure of "faculty power" that demanded increased participation in institutional decision-making. Although sometimes resisted by traditional administrations, the virtual explosion of institutional interests and concerns relating to faculty, students, finances, and physical facilities meant that there were more than enough academic and administrative responsibilities to occupy the attention of all interested participants. Various university senate, faculty council, and administrative systems were devised to comprehend this participatory decision-making. The actual exercise of such responsibility at a high level often was a sobering experience for professors whose view of administration may have been oversimplified. At any rate, the decade was an era of rising prestige, higher salaries, increased staff benefits, and greater mobility for faculty members. Disciplinary allegiance rivaled and often exceeded that for the institutions that hired the professors.

The 1960's and the Students

The seal of the 1960's on higher education bears the indelible

---

[36] Fred M. Hechinger, "Suddenly Ph.D.'s Are 'A Glut on the Market,' " *The New York Times,* Jan 4, 1970, p. 9E.

stamp of the students. They not only marched onto the campuses in massed millions, but they sought, seized, and exercised power in a fashion unique at least upon the American scene. They soon protested and later lashed out at the conditions they decried. They objected to crowded facilities, absentee or nonteaching professors, insensitive administrations, the pressure for grades, and the lock-step curricular requirements in many programs. They felt imprisoned by departmental requirements that reflected academic imperialism and presumed to seek for "relevance" in their studies to the real-life situations they faced. They railed at computerization and the depersonalization of their college experience. On the one hand, they cried out for closer student-teacher relations; on the other hand, they often disdained advice or instructions from their professors. They tended to denigrate the past and its experience and to focus only upon the present. Perhaps even more aggressively than faculties, they sought "student power" that would give them a voice in the decision-making apparatus of an institution. They gained places on important campus committees and bargained with deans, provosts, chancellors, and presidents over what often were presented as "nonnegotiable demands." They demanded and sometimes gained representation on boards of directors and trustees, and even began to share in the hiring and firing of faculty members in some institutions. They struck out against the *in loco parentis* concept, historically exercised by American institutions of higher education, especially in relation to student living arrangements. They grasped for the trappings of adulthood in respect to privileges and powers.

Large numbers of students identified with the idealism they perceived in the civil rights movement and the amelioration of racism. They undertook summer marches to the South, especially in Mississippi in 1964, on the civil rights trail. Early in the 1960's, many students took leaves of absence to do stints in the Peace Corps, and others, increasingly in the rest of the decade, undertook active social action roles in tutoring and counseling disadvantaged students, ranging from elementary through college levels. In 1969, one such student-initiated project, dubbed "The Cincinnati Experience," was operated with the cooperation of the University of Cincinnati and involved the active participation of some 500 students. Arrangements were made for the students in this community-participation project to receive college credit in the area of communications. It was given recognition on a national level by former Secretary Robert Finch,

Department of Health, Education, and Welfare, in the Nixon Cabinet, and was reported favorably in the national press.

There is no question but that student pressures were recognized and that they did bring about change in higher education. In addition to Black Studies, other innovations included the designation of courses to be given on pass-fail or other ungraded bases, more interdisciplinary majors, various honors courses, independent study programs, and brief interim or post-academic-year terms of about one month's duration for directed readings, study, or travel on a credit basis. Some institutions installed a Master of Arts for Teachers degree program that deemphasized research and stressed teacher preparation, and comparable doctorates were under consideration at the end of the 1960's. The traditional lecture-discussion techniques were enriched greatly by the use of a profusion of audio-visual and other instructional materials. These and other significant changes might have come anyway, but their appearance was facilitated greatly by student pressures.

There was also a negative side to the student picture in the 1960's that deserves attention. After the harsh reception in the South of students who joined civil rights marches in Alabama and Mississippi in 1964, many marchers returned in disillusionment to their campuses. Various radical groups sprung up that sought to take out their animus against society in general on the universities as the institutions in the social system with which they were most familiar, were closest at hand, and were exceedingly vulnerable to attack. The Students for a Democratic Society (SDS) was the most significant of such organizations. Its followers held that the system or "establishment" was so bad that it should be destroyed, even though they admittedly had nothing constructive to replace it. The SDS members, mostly recruited from affluent white middle-class groups, sought to ally with such black student groups as existed on the various campuses. On occasion, the blacks welcomed such aid, but, over the long run, they generally elected to direct their own protest programs. The "free-speech" movement first erupted into violence on the Berkeley campus of the University of California in 1964. The tempo of trouble accelerated in the succeeding years with protests occurring on hundreds of campuses that involved "demands" upon the institutions, "sit-ins" in administrative and other buildings, seizure of records, attacks upon personnel recruiters for the military services and defense-oriented industries, anti-ROTC views, and demands for immediate recruitment of additional black faculty, staff, and students. These incidents became increasingly violent, and sometimes were accompanied by attacks upon institutional officers, burning of buildings, and defiance of the authority of police and courts. Severe campus disturbances sometimes erupted when the cities were the scene of large-scale rioting, especially in the 1966-69 period. Shocking examples of student violence occurred on the Columbia, Harvard, and Cornell campuses in 1969; in the latter instance, the rioters were armed. The nation was shaken by these violent episodes, and the institutions, as well as their administrations and faculties, came in for heavy criticism. Congress authorized withdrawal of Federal financial aid from rioters, and state and national leaders were critical of college presidents for not cracking down on the rioters with force. Nevertheless, there was tacit agreement that the colleges should be given a chance to put their houses in order if possible without outside interference, especially by the police. The 1969-70 academic year started off with a seeming decline in campus unrest, and many hoped that the pendulum of student opinion had swung against the radicals and that peace on campus had a chance to prevail.

It should be stressed that neither the student protestors nor the social action groups commanded anything like majority support among their student bodies. On the other hand, their aggressive leadership and identification with causes of the moment often did secure either silence or support from the majority. As the decade wore on, however, evidence increased to indicate that the bulk of students were disenchanted with the rioters and protestors and wanted nothing more than to complete their educations and get on with the normal business of life.

Rationale for Unrest and Violence in the 1960's

Amazement, shock, anger, repression, submissive tolerance, and reasoned analysis all have been reactions on the part of millions of Americans who hardly could believe the events that transpired in the violent 1960's. To be sure, our history is replete with episodes and periods of violence, but to experience in the 1960's such extremes of disorder as arson, rioting, and near-guerrilla warfare on a large scale was more than most Americans could comprehend. Why should it have been so? Many able minds have pondered this problem, and this writer presumes no omniscience on the subject. Even so, some observations that reflect not only his own views, but the distillation of the thoughts of many others, may be helpful.

In the first place, to paraphrase sociologist-columnist Max Lerner, the role of the great American dream must be understood. Implicit in the American system throughout our history has been the belief that motivation, hard work, and education were channels by which underprivileged minority groups and persons could attain success and freedom from the ghetto; this was the dream. So long as these channels of progress were open, the minorities were content to work within the system.

Hope of success and the example of others who had achieved it were priceless ingredients in the social mix. With the prime exception of the blacks, this concept of the American dream had worked over the decades for the Irish, the Jews, and numerous other immigrant groups. As poverty was overcome, racial or ethnic prejudice generally declined. The "melting pot" not only made Americans, but it permitted them an opportunity—or at least the hope—for prosperity.

By 1939, much social progress had been made, but of course there remained much room for improvement. Beginning with 1940, there set in a period of 20-25 years when top priority, seemingly in the national interest, shifted from domestic progress to national defense and later the over-all security of the nation *vis á vis* the outside world. World War II soon was succeeded by the Korean conflict, and, concurrently, there arose the malevolent shadow of atomic warfare that threatened not only peace, but even human survival. Containment, massive retaliation, and monolithic communism were concepts of the 1950's that forced domestic issues into the background. Subconsciously, men ceded first place to national over internal security for persons and groups. The early 1960's, with the Bay of Pigs fiasco and the Cuban missile crisis, projected the same understanding into the new decade.

By 1964-65, however, the gamesmanship of international relations had undergone seemingly significant changes. Asian rumblings in the late 1950's and early 1960's anticipated a rift between Communist China and the U.S.S.R.; by 1963, it was clear that the communist monolith was fractured, and the assumption was that it no longer offered the potent threat of former years to the outside world. The Cuban crisis in 1962 had brought the great powers face to face with the awesome hazard of nuclear war, and the circling giants had backed away from atomic conflict. A limited nuclear test ban treaty even was negotiated. Conventional and guerrilla warfare were not outmoded, but was it true that the danger of nuclear annihilation had receded? Many Americans seemed to think so and breathed easier. As concern over international communism abated for other reasons as well, the validity of Vietnam as a focal point of American security came under increasing debate. Much discussion ensued over the extent to which defense expenditures delayed increasingly vital social and educational programs at home. Finally, by the 1960's, few among the younger Americans remembered or cared about the legacy of World War II, or even Korea. In short, by the mid-1960's, the unwritten contract the nation had with its minority groups to postpone adequate social and racial redress until the external threats were contained had fallen apart. This is not to suggest that significant progress in social amelioration had not been made since 1940, because much had been achieved. As had occurred in prerevolutionary periods in other lands, however, the demands of the have-not groups rose as they began to make significant gains, and they began to display great impatience. In the case of the blacks, the military services had offered opportunity for status and success to many men who had never known them before. Migration to the North, increased earnings in the cities, and some educational advances prepared many blacks for leadership roles in the 1960's. Still, there were millions of citizens who, as yet, shared very little in the outpouring of the American horn of plenty. After some 30 years of holding back, many had begun to lose hope that they would share in the American dream. When the security contract bonds were unwrapped in the mid-1960's, the pressures for reform and change were tremendous. It is important also to recognize the impact of the mass media, especially television, as vehicles for implanting the concept of instant gratification in the mind of the deprived person. Commercial advertising over television transmitted to millions of poor people the psychology that the material things of life were easily and instantly available—one only had to reach out and take them! In the civil rights area, the harsh reception given to marchers in Mississippi and Alabama convinced many that only violence would force the "establishment" to make changes. The nation then suffered through a series of "long, hot summers," that began in 1964 and lasted through 1968. In 1967, there were some 50 major riots that resulted in nearly 100 deaths and over $750,000,000 in property damages.

In addition to the above influences, student ideas and conduct in the 1960's were affected by other factors. Parents must share responsibility with their offspring for the attitudes and activities of the latter in the 1960's. In the main, these were parents who remembered the depression 1930's, survived the ordeal of World War II, strove for economic betterment, highly respected collegiate education, and determined that their children would be spared the hardships they had experienced. Permissiveness was the fad in the psychology of child rearing. Many children played the permissive game with their parents so successfully that they came to expect their wishes to be met immediately and without dispute—instant gratification. They learned the art of parent and people manipulation to obtain their desires, whether or not they were appropriate. The increasingly affluent lavished on their loved ones all of the material things that they themselves often had been denied in their youth. Thus, adolescents often were deprived of the conditioning influences of discipline, deferred rewards, persistence, and hard work in the struggle for success. Emerging victorious from succeeding rounds of debate with their parents, they saw little reason why others—college professors and administrators—should dispute their analyses and conclusions on problems as they saw them. Many children, despite an affluent environment, were bereft not only of guidance, but even presence or companionship in cases of broken homes or parental neglect. They observed the lip service paid to high ideals and moral codes, but were disillusioned by what they perceived as hypocrisy in parental adherence to them. It is important to emphasize that these young people, in general, did not have to be concerned immediately about economic security or the material things of life. Taking them for granted as their right, they were ready for direct action to introduce the changes and reforms they regarded as necessary. They saw little reason to question their own appraisal of the problems and their answers to them.[37] In addition, by and large, they were intelligent and better-educated than their forebears. The one area in which their parents had pressured them was education, and great stress had been placed upon grades and academic achievement.

---

[37] John W. Aldridge, "In the Country of the Young," *Harper's Magazine*, 239:49-64, October, 1969; Joseph Kraft, "How U.S. Escaped Historic Trap," *The Cincinnati Post & Times-Star*, Jan. 7, 1970.

There was another segment of students who were, in the words of Pres. Kingman Brewster, Jr., of Yale, involuntary college students. They either were refugees from the military draft or were in college in reflection of social pressure. Thus, a significant portion of college enrollees had an involuntary academic servitude enforced upon them that extended beyond adolescence for years and was resented. The view was that, if they had to be in the university, they wanted to control it.[38] Finally, there were the disadvantaged, disgruntled, and disillusioned blacks, who writhed under the impact of 300 years of discrimination and now seemed determined to have reparation made in one decade. These were some of the factors that lay behind the student unrest and often violent protest in the 1960's.

On the other hand, a large portion, perhaps the majority, of the students pursued their degree objectives with diligence and respectful behavior that seemed traditional and correct to their parents and professors. Also, it must be observed that many of the radical students were irrational, sometimes naive, often uninformed, disdainful of historical facts, deliberately deceptive in their strategies, and practioners of hypocrisy themselves. They usually were endowed with, and enjoyed the use of, the material things for which they criticized their parents and society so severely. By the end of the decade, the silent student majority was exercising some restraint on the radicals, college faculties and administrations were taking tougher stands, legislators and governors were threatening reprisals on institutions that failed to set their houses in order, and the influence of the Federal government also was being exercised on behalf of peace on the campuses. What the 1970's would bring was unknown, but the colleges and universities were enjoying a much-needed res- pite from unrest and violence at the close of the 1960's.

The Enrollment Explosion in the 1960's

The virtual explosion in student enrollments in the 1960's was in part reflective of the high birthrate years of the late 1940's and may be summarized here. In 1960-61, the big news was a fulltime freshman increase of 11.4% over 1959-60, with a total of 495,269 freshmen counted comparably in the categories surveyed. This number was surprising in view of the low birthrate in the World War II years,

---

[38] " 'Pressures Force Too Many to Go to College' says Yale's Brewster," *The Chronicle of Higher Education,* Jan. 5, 1970, p. 4.

from which this class was derived. In all 1,016 institutions—1960-61 being the first year in which the report covered more than 1,000 schools—there were 2,039,854 full-time students and a grand total of 2,942,571; as compared to 1959-60, the increases were 6.2% and 5.5%.[39] Full-time students led the enrollment flock in 1961-62, when there were 2,257,921 students in 1,047 comparably reporting accredited institutions, for an increase of 7.5% over 1960-61. The grand total count was 3,215,427, a rise of 6.6%, in comparable schools; this was the first year the accredited institutions enrolled over 3,000,000 students. Freshman enrollments increased by only 5.4%, lower than the 11.4% of 1960-61, and an indication that the big bulge in freshmen was yet to come. Some discernment of current problems was reflected in the author's observation that, "In these days of atomic fall-out fear, concern over internal dissent, and problems with the uncommitted neutral nations of the world, there is a clamant need for level heads and trained minds." He went on to hope that "the disciplines of the arts and sciences will contribute to that reservoir of ideas, experience, and good judgment that will help us to preserve and strengthen our free society."[40] He still had that hope in 1970, but it was shaken somewhat by the stressful years of the later 1960's. After some years of increases, freshman enrollments in engineering and business administration showed slight declines of less than one per cent each. It was suggested that this reflected, in part, "the new glamor in mathematics and the pure sciences that derives in part from the psychology of the missile age." Emphasis was placed upon the National Education Association's estimate that nearly 350,000 new full-time college teachers would be needed in the 1959-70 period, and the author anticipated that "not only training, but the recruitment of qualified teachers will be one of the great educational challenges of the decade of the 1960's. . . .," and it was.[41] The year 1962-63 marked the 10th straight year of collegiate enrollment increases, and returns from 1,090 accredited institutions showed 2,455,398 full-time students and a grand total of 3,492,626, for respective increases of 6.2% and 6.5% in comparable units. Freshman enrollments only rose by .3%, but this had been expected,

---

[39] Garland G. Parker, "Statistics of Attendance in American Universities and Colleges, 1960-61," *School & Society*, 89:2184, Jan. 14, 1961, pp. 3-18.

[40] Garland G. Parker, "Statistics of Attendance in American Universities and Colleges, 1961-62," *School & Society*, 90:2202, Jan. 13, 1962, pp. 5-6.

[41] *Ibid.*, pp. 19-20.

since new entrants still were coming out of low birthrate years during World War II. The writer indicated, however, that this was the lull before the academic storm, because "an enormous corps of potential full-time students is being prepared in the high schools for admission to college two or three years hence." Also, he suggested that the need for projects and policies "to encourage more qualified persons to enter teaching, to accelerate their preparation, to render their teaching more effective, and to utilize their services more efficiently are in order for these times." He referred to mechanical teaching aids, closed-circuit television, programmed courses, independent and directed study, purging of nonessential courses from the curriculum, and a more-generous granting of credit by examination as concepts that deserved attention.[42]

In 1963-64, freshmen rose by 3.8%, but the author anticipated rises of 20% and 12.5% in the two years to follow, and warned that, if the "academic, physical, and financial resources to take care of this host of expected collegians are not already in a state of preparation, it is too late." Full-time students moved up by 6.4% and grand total students by 6.3%; in all, there were 2,594,519 and 3,702,331 students in the respective categories. Attention was called to the fact that "the teachers college label is not so meaningful as it once was," since many such colleges, perhaps regrettably, elected to drop the name in favor of more comprehensive titles, "but are still essentially teacher training institutions." A 20% growth in junior college enrollments was noted. In respect to college teachers, it was observed that only 25.4% held doctorates in 1962, as compared to 31.4% in 1953. Competition with industry and government for personnel and the need for higher salaries for teachers were stressed.[43]

The year of the freshman was 1964-65, when his number increased 17.3% in the accredited institutions and approached 20% across the country. All subject matter areas tabulated showed massive increases in freshmen that year, but of particular interest was the rise of 18% in teacher training programs, in view of the critical need for teachers that then prevailed. Full-time students numbered 2,909,638 students in 1,111 accredited institutions and the grand total was

[42] Garland G. Parker, "Statistics of Attendance in American Universities and Colleges, 1962-63," *School & Society*, 91:2219, Jan. 12, 1963, pp. 5-21.

[43] Garland G. Parker, "Statistics of Attendance in American Universities and Colleges, 1963-64," *School & Society*, 92:2236, Jan. 11, 1964, pp. 5-18.

4,118,735, for rises of 10.1% and 9.3% in comparable schools. These truly were massive gains, and it was a tribute to the machinery of higher education that they could be accommodated at all. It is little wonder that there were many complications arising from the arrival of such numbers on our college campuses.[44]

In 1965-66, freshmen rolled up still another 17.3% increase, the same as the previous year, despite the fact that the 18-year-old population increase was no more than 10-12% over 1964-65. Explanations for this spectacular freshman performance were rising social and economic pressures, increased financial aid, an increasingly affluent society, and the increase in educational opportunities, *i.e.,* places in college for students. Grand total enrollments rose by 10% and full-time numbers grew by 12.7%, record rises even over the previous year and the highest of the decade. In his comments on the "leviathans of academia—the big 30," the author warned that anonymity and depersonalization of students in such institutions "should be avoided at all costs. If not, we may expect students to lash out at the imaginary educational giant which constricts, isolates, and depersonalizes them. In their classes, departments, personnel and counseling arrangements, and social groups the students must be assured of vital and personal relationships that generate a sense of involvement, responsibility, and self-respect. Above all, students yearn for a close personal rapport with their professors and feel educationally and intellectually deprived without it. Perhaps the 'publish or perish' syndrome can be complemented with a 'relate or regret' concept." The author still regards these observations as sound.[45]

Still higher counts were reported in 1,108 reporting institutions in 1966-67 with 3,580,612 full-time students and 4,882,211 grand total enrollees—increases of eight per cent and 5.8%, respectively, in comparable situations. For the first time since 1951, however, full-time freshmen were down, with a decrease of .9%; but, when account was taken of junior college entrants, the total number probably was higher than for 1965-66. The impact of Selective Service and the fact that most freshmen were born in 1948, a low birthrate year, were reasons for the decrease in the accredited schools. Attention was called to the distending enrollments then in the middle college years

---

[44] Garland G. Parker, "Statistics of Attendance in American Universities and Colleges, 1964-65," *School & Society,* 93:2253, Jan. 9, 1965, pp. 5-20.

[45] Garland G. Parker, "Statistics of Attendance in American Universities and Colleges, 1965-66," *School & Society,* 94:2270, Jan. 8, 1966, pp. 7-22.

in reflection of the two large freshman classes in the two previous years.[46]

For 1967-68, 1,132 schools reported 3,854,645 full-time and 5,219,-218 grand total students—gains in comparable schools of 6.2% and 5.7%. Freshmen resumed their rise pattern again, with a 2.3% increase. Military service, the distraction of internal strife, competition of noncollegiate training programs, and the fact that there were fewer 18-year-olds in the country than in 1966-67 accounted for the slackening of freshman enrollments. Special emphasis in this report was given to the need for the involvement of urban institutions in the life and problems of the communities around them.[47]

Reports from 1,145 institutions in 1968-69 showed 4,092,234 full-time students (the first time the 4,000,000 mark was exceeded), and there were 5,521,963 grand total registrants; in comparable schools, the increases were the same in each category, 6.2%.[48]

The annual *School & Society* report for the closing year of the decade, 1969-70, and the 50th in the series inaugurated by Dr. Raymond Walters in 1919, comprehended 1,145 accredited universities, senior colleges, four-year colleges, and two-year schools administered by institutions in the above categories. This was the same number of schools reporting in 1968-69, and the full-time enrollment was 4,156,268 and the grand total 5,744,335. The comparable schools had a full-time increase of 4.8%, and the grand total rise was 4.6%. The freshman increase in 948 comparable institutions was 4.5%, and the total number in the categories surveyed was 922,111. Nursing majors, for the first time, showed the largest freshman percentage increase, 7.5%, followed by education, agriculture, arts and sciences, and business administration, in that order. Engineers only rose by .1%, and the outlook was not bright for their increase in the years to follow. Although the U.S. Office of Education report was unavailable at this writing, it was estimated that the total enrollment of all higher education students in some 2,500 institutions would approach 7,980,000. Attention was called to the leveling-off, and even a slight decline, in the number of 18-year-olds in the 1970's. The estimate was that enrollments would continue to increase through that de-

---

[46] Garland G. Parker, "Statistics of Attendance in American Universities and Colleges, 1966-67," *School & Society*, 95:2285, Jan. 7, 1967, pp. 9-24.

[47] Garland G. Parker, "Statistics of Attendance in American Universities and Colleges, 1967-68," *School & Society*, 96:2300, Jan. 6, 1968, pp. 9-24.

[48] Garland G. Parker, "Statistics of Attendance in American Universities and Colleges, 1968-69," *School & Society*, 97:2314, January, 1969, pp. 43-61.

cade, but there was the possibility of a decline in the early 1980's. It seemed clear, however, that the higher education system faced at least another decade of massive enrollments. It was to be expected that additional challenges and changes lay ahead that would deserve the serious attention and vigorous support of the nation as it endeavored to see that its young people would be able to have adequate educational opportunity.[49]

The Legacy of the 1960's

Most observers who attempted decade-end reviews of the 1960's came out with dreary ones that dwelled upon the dissent, unrest, domestic violence, and international conflict of that turbulent era. Unquestionably, there was a basis for deep concern over events of the decade. Indeed, this writer, in an earlier section, pursued no Pollyanna approach, but there was another face of the 1960's that deserves examination. The bent of the news media, the intellectuals, and the populace, by and large, was to focus upon the negative, critical, and cynical, and to neglect the positive, constructive, and optimistic factors in the picture. Solid achievement so often was taken for granted and not regarded as newsworthy. Even the Presidential recounting of positive accomplishments in a press conference often was looked upon as a "laundry list" that smacked of boasting and therefore was to be disregarded. Many prophets viewed with alarm our national errors and shortcomings and stressed the failure to solve in 10 years many problems that had perplexed our people for centuries. In fact, the progress of the decade was impressive. There was concern about poor people in 1970, but the number of people living on the edge of poverty in 1969 was only about half of the 40,000,000 there in 1960. That the number on welfare rose sharply reflected, in part, the fact that more persons were receiving aid, many of whom had needed it all along.[50] The affluent, mostly white, middle class prospered. By 1968, their disposable income in constant dollars, allowing for inflation, had increased 30% over 1960 and at a rate more than twice as fast as had been the case in the 1950's. Nonwhite families in 1968 earned 63% as much as white families, compared to 52% in 1959. From 1961 to 1969, the unemployment

---

[49] Garland G. Parker, "Statistics of Attendance in American Universities and Colleges, 1969-70," *School & Society,* 98:2322, January, 1970, pp. 41-58.

[50] Ben J. Wattenberg, "Irony Characterizes Decade of Change," *Cincinnati Enquirer,* Dec. 28, 1969.

rate declined from a high of 6.7% to 3.7% in September of the latter year; in numbers the decrease was from 4,714,000 to 2,958,000, while the labor force increased by 11,000,000. The proportion of people in white-collar jobs increased from 43% to 46% in the 1960-68 period, and the nonwhite rise was from 16% to 24%. In blue-collar jobs, the nonwhite increase was 57% and the whites rose by 12%. Throughout the decade, the proportion of nonwhites in substandard housing was reduced by almost half from the 25% in 1960. As reflected in the annual *School & Society* enrollment reports and this chapter, the measurable progress in education was most impressive. Moreover, the percentage of young people completing high school rose from approximately 54% in 1950 to 61% in 1960 and 73% in 1968. In 1960, the percentage of 18-19-year-olds in colleges was about 38%, but reached about 53% in 1969.[51] Meanwhile, absolute numbers of enrollees in institutions of higher education were growing from 3,471,000 in 1959-60 to some 7,980,000 or more in 1969-70, an increase of 129.9%.[52] Attention already has been given to the fantastic achievement of the higher education apparatus in absorbing this massive student increase. Federal funds for support of education in all aspects rose from some $2,000,000,000 in 1960 to $9,000,000,000 in 1969. Meanwhile, from 1964 to 1968, a whole new code of laws, both Federal and state, was addressed to "reordering the basis for relationships between black and white citizens in America. . . ."[53] The 1960's was a time when serious racial and other problems surfaced, and the nation was in great travail. It was forced to call heavily upon its reserves in terms of energy, ingenuity, patience, social concern, legal remedies, and constitutional resources. To permit appropriate pressures and experimentation, on the one hand, and to protect its democratic institutions and the freedom of its people, on the other, posed a desperate dilemma for the nation. That so much progress was made in solving problems was important, but of greater significance was the fact that they were met head-on, and not evaded. As the rest of the world watched in weird fascination, this mighty nation engaged in a mortal struggle with itself to determine whether or not the great American dream could be shared appropriately with its various population groups,

[51] *Ibid.*

[52] *A Fact Book on Higher Education,* First Issue, (Washington: American Council on Education, 1969), p. 9022.

[53] Wattenberg, *op. cit.*

especially the ethnic minorities, and, at the same time, if its democratic procedures reflected in representative government could be preserved and even strengthened. The legacy of the 1960's, thus, was one of monumental achievements counterbalanced by ponderous problems that awaited solutions in the 1970's.

6. Features for Fifty Years

The Enrollment Kaleidoscope

SOME ENROLLMENT features that transcend all 50 years, and others that appear only once or intermittently, merit attention here. With some nostalgia, we may reflect upon an earlier era when the pace of life, a lesser population, lower enrollments, and fewer institutions permitted a more leisurely reporting on enrollments and related aspects of higher education than now is possible. At the outset, with attention focused upon only 30 "representative" institutions, it was possible for the author to delve into the enrollment details that often were interesting and revealing. In the years from 1919-20 through 1946-47, the last year for which separate treatment was accorded the 30 institutions as a group, there is a collage of valuable information that comprehends enrollments and educational trends in summer schools, dentistry, law, medicine, graduate work, liberal arts, agriculture, business administration, veterinary medicine, engineering, architecture, fine arts, and other areas.[54] This study does not compre-

---

[54] The 30 "representative" universities were California, Chicago, Cincinnati, Columbia, Cornell, Harvard, Illinois, Indiana, University of Iowa, Johns Hopkins, Kansas, Michigan, Minnesota, Missouri, Nebraska, Northwestern, Ohio State, University of Pennsylvania, Pittsburgh, Princeton, Stanford, Syracuse, Texas, Tulane, University of Washington (replaced New York University in 1921-22), Virginia, Washington University, Western Reserve (now Case-Western Reserve University), Wisconsin, and Yale.

hend detailed analysis of such material, but some aspects of it will be given attention.

Miscellany

References in the early reports to Leland Stanford Junior University looked strange in 1970, but it was not until 1925-26 that, at its own request, the institution was referred to as Stanford University. In 1919-20, it was noted that five of the 30 institutions—Yale, Princeton, Cincinnati, Washington University, and Western Reserve—did not then have summer schools, It is a fact, however, that the reports provide a valuable reservoir of information on summer school enrollments through 1947-48. In the same year, 1919-20, Harvard University registration figures were available only for the whole year, and those for Indiana University covered the entire semester, rather than the count for Nov. 1. Attention was called to the fact that "a general plan for the limitation of students at Princeton is shortly to be presented by the faculty to the trustees." This was the first of many references to moves by numerous institutions to limit enrollments. No doubt such policies did have a restricting effect on enrollments, but, in almost every such case, student numbers later continued to creep upward. It is also of interest to see references in 1922-23, and for some years thereafter, to the Junior College Department, Southern Branch, at Los Angeles (established in 1919), when enrollments were cited for the University of California.[55] It was not until 1928-29 that the institution, at its request, was referred to as the University of California at Los Angeles (UCLA). The Southern Branch, it was noted in 1923-24, had "a separate faculty which administers its own affairs, subject to the policies and broader regulations developed at the older seat of the university at Berkeley. Instruction at the Southern Branch is provided in a four-year course leading to the degree of bachelor of education and also in academic curricula covering freshman, sophomore and junior work. Next year the fourth year of undergraduate instruction will be offered in Los Angeles." Degree-credit students at the Southern Branch in 1923-24 numbered 2,649,[56] in comparison to 30,936 in 1969-70. In 1926-27, note was taken of

---

[55] Raymond Walters, "Statistics of Registration in American Universities and Colleges, 1921," *School & Society*, 15:373, Feb. 18, 1922, pp. 181-184.

[56] Raymond Walters, "Statistics of Registration in American Universities and Colleges, 1924," *School & Society*, 19:477, Feb. 16, 1924, p. 175.

"President Splawn's recent statement prepared for *School and Society* to the effect that the University of Texas is to receive royalties on about 8,000,000 barrels of oil, which is the estimated yield in the next fifteen or twenty years from an oil pool on land owned by the university. This oil is now selling at something more than $1.80 a barrel. The university has already received about $2,000,000 as royalty. The supreme court of the state will decide whether the money is to be placed in the building fund of the university or to be added to the permanent endowment. Architects estimate that the proposed building program will cost $10,000,000."[57] In accounting for 876 freshman students at Yale in 1926-27, it was explained that their work was preparatory both for Yale College and Sheffield Scientific School and also comprehended 42 students in nursing and "87 in the drama course of Professor Baker."[58] Such were some of the details in the early Walters reports.

From Manual to Machine Records

In no aspect of higher education has there been a more revolutionary development than the areas of records systems and management. In earlier days, enrollment and other higher education records were collected, maintained, and reported manually. As late as the early 1950's, some institutions still were using pen, India ink, and translucent paper stock for recording grades on permanent records, and statistics were kept by hand and tabulated manually in most institutions through the 1940's. In many instances, manual procedures continued even into the 1960's. To report the retention of hand operations is not necessarily to denigrate them. So long as time, smaller numbers, and less sophisticated data requirements permitted, manually produced records had high accuracy, were subject to simple revision, usually were quickly available, and were economical to produce. As enrollments multiplied and data needs became increasingly complicated, other techniques became mandatory.

Adding machines, desk calculators, typewriters, punched cards penetrated by hand-directed needles to facilitate sorting, and various copiers were among the earlier mechanical aids in the handling of

---

[57] Raymond Walters, "Statistics of Registration in American Universities and Colleges, 1925," *School & Society*, 23:578, Jan. 23, 1926, p. 97.

[58] Raymond Walters, "Statistics of Registration in American Universities and Colleges, 1926," *School & Society*, 25:628, Jan. 8, 1927, p. 32.

registration records. By the late 1930's and in the 1940's, many institutions began to use mechanical equipment for processing key-punched cards in the maintenance of student and other records. University business offices frequently pioneered in the field of "machine records." As noted earlier, there was virtually a mass movement of institutions to the use of machine equipment for records maintenance in the 1950's, and the rapid rise of computers was a prime characteristic of the 1960's. The impact of machine-produced records and computer technology upon higher education was tremendous, especially as it affected registrars and other reporting officers. By the 1950's, the operation and management of data processing equipment had created a whole new profession. Those university staff members that shunned the new technology generally fell by the wayside in professional growth. The registrars and admissions officers who learned how to communicate with machine records and computer experts and recognized the value of mechanically produced data reports as management-information tools often rose in stature to become deans of admissions and records, vice provosts, vice presidents, and the like. In many other cases, such officers stagnated or declined in status and service capacity within their institutions. Meanwhile, new administrative posts—such as supervisors of data processing and computer center directors—appeared on organization charts.

In academic areas, especially in the physical and biological sciences, but increasingly in almost all other disciplines as well, computer technology became the strong right arm of research. The plotting of planet orbits, satellite itineraries, and spaceship journeys was made practicable by the computer. As in the case of administrators, faculty members had to make their peace with the computer in research areas or be dubbed as "traditional," "conventional," or "conservative" scholars by the younger staff members. In collegiate administration, the computer brought deliverance from the desperate dearth of data from which collegiate administrators long had suffered, and gave rise to virtually a new science of institutional management. By the end of the decade, a so-called Planned Program Budgeting System (PPBS), involving quantification of institutional objectives and programs wherever possible, and made possible by computer operations, was the new approach to academic and institutional planning.

Along with the boon of a massive data base, computers also

brought problems. Staffing computer centers with trained operators, programmers, and systems experts required a never-ceasing search for personnel. It was a particular problem to recruit computer experts who possessed an appropriate understanding of, and were sensitive to, the peculiar relationships pervading most academic communities. In addition, partly in reflection of personnel scarcity, but also of the overly aggressive sales techniques of some computer salesmen and their companies, unrealistic planning often occurred. Machine "hardware" too frequently was placed on the market before adequate "software" in terms of systems and programs was available for satisfactory operation. Also, despite their incredible speed in mass-producing desirable data, computers had an enormous capacity for error. Thus, major mistakes made with fantastic speed on occasion invalidated data and jeopardized decision-making with sometimes disastrous results. Also, a seemingly inordinate amount of time was consumed in devising systems to produce desired data, writing programs in languages the computer could interpret, accomplishing data input, and, finally, getting "on" the computer to run a program. The irony of records computerization was the frequent delays in producing reports. The enrollment pollster, particularly, was aware of this lag in data reporting. Over and over again, he was told that delayed reports, or no reports at all, were caused by computer problems. Institutional management locally and in statewide systems was handicapped severely in academic and budgetary planning for the next year, or the forthcoming biennium, when enrollment and other reports were not available on time. Another problem was that of finance. Computer systems were very expensive and often were employed without adequate costing knowledge prior to their purchase or rental and use on specific applications. At the end of the 1960's, an expense of from one to several millions of dollars per year for a single installation was not uncommon. In the later 1960's, this writer often was highly critical of data deficiencies attributed to computer problems. This criticism was justified and deserved expression, but simultaneously it was recognized that the computer was indispensable in modern record-keeping. Indeed, the author was a strong supporter of the proper application of computer technology to data reporting and problem-solving in the field of higher education. A host of other machine-related techniques for improving data input and output appeared in the 50 years under review, but space limitations preclude their consideration here.

TABLE I

STUDENT ENROLLMENTS BY DECADES, 1919-20 TO 1969-70

Categories	1919-20	1929-30	1939-40	1949-50	1959-60	1969-70
Students in 30 "Representative Universities"**	(30)	(30)	(30)	(30)	(30)	(30)
Full-time	147,274	193,709	233,262	387,812	368,621	711,945
Grand Total	183,459	320,494	349,445	484,711	504,864	896,471
Students in Approved or Accredited Institutions*		(224)	(648)	(753)	(995)	(1,145)
Full-time	.....	433,253	873,697	1,567,500	1,973,948	4,156,268
Grand Total	.....	687,855	1,323,874	1,994,795	2,811,704	5,744,335
Grand Total Students in All Institutions†	(1,041)	(1,409)	(1,708)	(1,851)	(1,952)	
	597,880	1,100,737	1,494,203	2,659,021	3,402,297	.....

* SCHOOL & SOCIETY enrollment articles.
† U. S. Office of Education reports.

TABLE II

FRESHMAN ENROLLMENTS BY FIELDS*

1934-35 In 487 Institutions		%
Liberal Arts	112,106	72.2
Engineering	20,283	13.1
Commerce	16,553	10.7
Agriculture	6,270	4.0
Totals	155,212	

1939-40 In 623 Institutions		%
Liberal Arts	150,642	59.2
Engineering	37,799	14.9
Commerce	23,574	9.3
Agriculture	10,950	4.3
Teachers	31,572	12.4
Totals	254,537	

1949-50 No Report on Freshmen

1959-60 In 845 Institutions	Men	%	Women	%
Arts and Sciences	141,199	53.6	120,240	67.0
Engineering	52,175	19.8	680	.4
Commerce	29,649	11.3	9,177	5.1
Agriculture	8,457	3.2	1,400	.8
Teachers	31,975	12.1	47,834	26.7
Totals	263,455		179,331	

1969-70 In 948 Institutions	Men	%	Women	%
Arts and Sciences	240,285	47.2	210,549	50.9
Engineering	59,300	11.7	1,594	.4
Business	57,263	11.3	15,768	3.8
Agriculture	11,758	2.3	2,581	.6
Education	32,376	6.4	79,192	19.2
Nursing	266		14,335	3.5
All Others	107,344	21.1	89,500	21.6
Totals	508,592		413,519	

* In 1934-35, 1939-40, and 1959-60 (no report on freshmen in 1949-50), the percentages only are related to the total freshmen in the reported categories and not to all freshmen. In 1969-70, the percentages are based on a requested reporting of all freshmen.

TABLE III
COMPARISON OF 30 REPRESENTATIVE INSTITUTIONS IN 1919-20 WITH BIG 30 IN 1969-70

30 Institutions, 1919-20†

University	1919 Enrollment Excluding Summer School	1919 Rank	University	1919 Enrollment Including Summer School	1919 Rank
New York Univ.	11,237	1	Columbia	15,828	1
California	9,435	2	California	12,609	2
Michigan	8,255	3	New York Univ.	12,017	3
Columbia	8,069	4	Chicago	9,816	4
Illinois	8,052	5	Michigan	9,171	5
Minnesota	7,451	6	Wisconsin	9,107	6
Pennsylvania	7,094	7	Illinois	8,752	7
Wisconsin	6,872	8	Minnesota	8,236	8
Northwestern	6,798	9	Pennsylvania	8,029	9
Ohio State	6,608	10	Cornell	7,868	10
Cornell	5,718	11	Northwestern	7,679	11
Chicago	5,602	12	Harvard	7,305	12
Harvard	5,273	13	Ohio State	7,224	13
Nebraska	4,245	14	Texas	5,276	14
Texas	4,099	15	Nebraska	4,791	15
Pittsburgh	4,085	16	Iowa Univ.	4,575	16
Syracuse	4,081	17	Pittsburgh	4,544	17
Iowa State	3,949	18	Syracuse	4,397	18
Kansas	3,580	19	Missouri	4,176	19
Missouri	3,346	20	Kansas	4,002	20
Cincinnati	3,326	21	Indiana	3,618	21
Indiana	2,930	22	Cincinnati*	3,346	22
Yale	2,633	23	Yale*	3,326	23
Johns Hopkins	2,441	24	Tulane	3,233	24
Stanford	2,356	25	Virginia	3,015	25
Tulane	2,182	26	Stanford	2,961	26
Washington Univ.	2,033	27	Johns Hopkins	2,844	27
Western Reserve	1,992	28	Washington U.*	2,033	28
Princeton	1,850	29	Western Reserve*	1,992	29
Virginia	1,541	30	Princeton*	1,850	30
Totals	**147,133**		**Totals**	**185,620**	

The Big 30 Institutions, 1969-70†
Largest Institutions (including component units)

Largest Institutions (including component units)	Full-time	Rank	Grand Total	Rank
State University of New York	179,107	1	286,707	1
The California State Colleges	139,100	2	265,537	2
The City Univ. of New York	83,053	3	167,302	3
The Wisconsin State University System	54,793	4	61,890	8
University of Texas System	51,661	5	64,572	7
University of Wisconsin	50,504	6	68,109	6
University of Minnesota	50,415	7	70,234	5
University of Illinois	46,292	8	54,076	9
Ohio State University	44,560	9	49,132	13
Indiana University	41,884	10	53,575	10
Michigan State University	39,244	11	50,085	11
University of Missouri	36,427	12	47,170	15
Pennsylvania State University	35,764	13	49,859	12
University of Maryland	35,537	14	48,203	14
University of North Carolina	34,757	15	40,923	16
University of Michigan	30,225	16	38,328	17
Southern Illinois University	27,871	17	36,446	20
University of Tennessee	27,408	18	36,320	21
Purdue University	27,226	19	36,888	19
University of Washington	26,909	20	32,749	26
Louisiana State University	25,355	21	32,601	27
Brigham Young University	22,139	22	—	—
Wayne State University	21,475	23	34,924	23
Kent State University	21,166	24	28,731	29
University of Massachusetts	20,395	25	35,174	22
University of Cincinnati	20,107	26	—	—
University of Colorado	20,032	27	31,096	28
Rutgers—The State University	19,460	28	—	—
University of Florida	19,211	29	—	—
Iowa State University	18,094	30	—	—
University of California*	—	—	106,274	4
Northeastern University	—	—	37,134	18
New York University	—	—	33,421	24
Temple University	—	—	32,973	25
University of Pittsburgh	—	—	28,426	30

* No summer school.
† Extracts from Tables II and III as printed in first Walters SCHOOL & SOCIETY report, 1919-20.

* Did not report full-time figures.
† Table 5 as printed in 1969-70 SCHOOL & SOCIETY report.

TABLE IV

FULL-TIME TEACHING STAFFS BY TYPE OF INSTITUTIONS

	1919-20	1929-30	1939-40	1949-50	1959-60	1969-70
Universities and Large Institutions of Complex Organization						
Public	(13) 6,891	(53) 17,734	(56) 22,899	(55) 28,925	(68) 45,957	(80) 88,154
Private	(14) 8,291	(36) 16,640	(51) 29,286	(48) 20,279	(56) 26,407	(61) 45,442
Independent Colleges of Arts & Sciences	*	(122) 7,608	(409) 21,783	(471) 27,829	(618) 40,308	(712) 68,210
Independent Schools of Technology and Related Schools	*	(12) 1,552	(51) 8,497	(53) 12,131	(63) 13,106	(77) 17,409
Independent Teachers Colleges	*	*	(72) 5,101	(113) 8,630	(147) 12,819	(148) 29,882
Fine Arts, Applied Arts, and Music	*	*	*	*	(13) 433	(19) 811
Theological Seminaries and Schools for Lay Workers	*	*	*	*	(13) 162	(32) 717
School and Society Totals	(27) 15,182	(223) 43,534	(639) 87,566	(740) 97,794	(978) 139,192	(1,129) 250,625
All U. S. Institutions†	(1,041) 48,615	(1,409) 82,386	(1,708) 146,929	(1,851) 246,722		

* Not reported.
† U. S. Office of Education.

Full-time Students and Scope of the Studies

As noted earlier, a major feature in the *School & Society* reports has been the distinction between full-time and part-time students. As emphasized in the annual reports, the basic assumption is that the full-time students—those who devote substantially all of their working time to their studies—comprise the heart of academe. This group has commanded prime consideration in academic, physical, and fiscal planning, and also has produced the main contingent of the nation's scientists, doctors, lawyers, engineers, business administrators, clergymen, pharmacists, teachers, nurses, and professionals, as well as leaders in many other fields. This emphasis has not denied the high importance of part-time students nor their valuable contributions in most arenas of public, private, and professional life. It simply stresses the fact that the full-time students have dominated the educational scene. Table I shows the full-time enrollments in the 30 representative institutions and the accredited schools at 10-year intervals.

In 1952-54, the U.S. Office of Education Biennial Survey accepted the principles of classification of institutions and distinction between full-time and part-time students, but such categories were not reported there regularly until the 1960's. The *School & Society* surveys covered the 30 "representative" schools from 1919-20 through 1946-47. Otherwise, since 1921-22, only the approved or accredited institutions have been comprehended in the studies. Given these limitations, however, this series not only is the oldest annual collegiate enrollment report, but provides the only comparable, comprehensive, and continuous registration records for full-time and part-time students in the accredited universities, senior colleges, four-year colleges, and the two-year schools administered by the institutions in the above-designated categories. As has been noted in the annual articles, the *School & Society* and the U.S. Office of Education opening fall enrollment reports are complementary. The former is selective in that it is restricted to the accredited schools; the latter is comprehensive in its coverage of all institutions of higher education. The results, therefore, may show similarities or differences without being contradictory. It is anticipated that a need will continue for a study of full-time enrollments based on the accredited institutions as defined in the *School & Society* studies.

The Totals Were Grand

Another significant measurement of enrollments is in grand totals. These comprise both full-time and part-time students, also reported by decades in Table I for the 30 representative schools, the accredited institutions, and all colleges and universities. The increases from 183,459 to 896,471, from 687,855 (in 1929-30) to 5,744,335, and from 597,880 to an estimated 7,980,000 in the respective categories certainly tell the story of statistical growth in higher education over the 50 years under review.

Freshmen to the Fore

Since 1934-35, the prime importance of freshman figures in anticipating trends and determining future enrollments has been recognized in the annual surveys. The colleges have to live with freshmen and their academic survivors throughout the normal collegiate span of years and on into professional and graduate school programs. Likewise, their study choices are important in shaping future curricular patterns. The authors of these studies have recognized the need for first-time degree-credit student counts as conducted by the U.S. Office of Education. To restrict freshman tabulations to such registrants, however, belies the fact that many students enter college in the winter, spring, and summer terms, or re-enter as freshman returnees. First-time degree-credit tabulations do not take account of these students, who are significant in number and have an important position in the statistical base from which later enrollments and earned degrees are derived. Freshmen reported for the *School & Society* surveys, therefore, have included all full-time persons classified as first-year or freshman undergraduate students, but they are not necessarily first-time degree-credit students. Practical limitations of staff, finance, time, and publication space have restricted the coverage of freshmen to the specific fields previously indicated. Nevertheless, these reports provide the only comparable and near-continuous records on freshman enrollments in the designated study areas. The writer understands that the counts are not definitive in the reports on freshmen in the specified fields, but the disparities probably are not statistically significant. Granted their limitations, it may be said on behalf of the *School & Society* studies that, in the designated areas, they are oases in a desert of freshman enrollment statistics that extended over the early decades of the half-century under review. Table II starts with 1934-35, and displays freshman enrollments thereafter on a decennial basis—except for 1949-50, when none were reported—by the stated study fields in the accredited institutions.

Enrollments by Disciplines

The classification by types of institutions initiated in 1932-33, and the reports on freshmen, since 1934-35, by study areas provide invaluable enrollment data for certain academic areas. There is no doubt that some students reported by the institutions in the various disciplinary categories were not majors in the areas indicated, but the numbers were indicative of some of the important academic emphases in the years surveyed. Because of the sweeping changes in nomenclature and administrative organization of institutions, the classifications were less meaningful, or perhaps had different meaning, by the end of the 1960's than in the 1930's. Nevertheless, they offer one of the few vantage points for viewing the passing parade of enrollments by school classifications and academic areas. Detailed analysis of the annual returns is not feasible here, but a comparison of the reports in the classified areas for 1939-40 and 1969-70 is of interest and illustrative of some of the changes over the years. In 1939-40, of 648 reporting institutions, the number of schools and full-time students in the various classifications were as follows: 56 large public universities, 275,685; 51 large private universities, 184,-766; 418 arts and sciences colleges, 239,618; 51 technological institutions, 99,686; 72 teachers colleges, 73,942; and the full-time student total was 873,697.[59] By 1969-70, the number of schools and full-time students reported in the various categories were as follows: 89 large public universities, 1,780,387; 64 large private universities, 501,792; 715 arts and sciences colleges, 1,123,604; 78 technological, professional, and related schools, 212,533; 148 teachers colleges, 509,858; 19 fine arts, applied arts, and music schools, 10,483; 32 theological seminaries and schools for lay workers, 5,842; and a total of 4,156,268 full-time students in 1,145 reporting institutions.[60]

---

[59] Raymond Walters, "Statistics of Registration in American Universities and Colleges, 1939," *School & Society*, 50:1303, Dec. 16, 1939, pp. 669-768.

[60] Garland G. Parker, "Statistics of Attendance in American Universities and Colleges, 1969-70," *School & Society*, 98:2322, January, 1970, pp. 41-58. The

Semantics are important in the prestige-conscious academic world, and this was evident in the decade of the 1960's, as institutions requested classification changes in the tabular listings. There was a scramble for coveted positions in the large public universities category. On the other hand, there was a flight from the teachers colleges and technological institutions classifications. While this reflected much realistic development of university and multiple-purpose college functions in many institutions, it was unfortunate to see by implication a denigration of teachers colleges and technological institutions. After all, these classes of schools have performed indispensable functions in society, and seemingly would deserve an accolade rather than downgrading. The Table II totals by category indicate decennial year enrollment trends in the subject matter areas elected by freshmen. Again, it is understood that there are discrepancies between the actual majors chosen by some students and the broad areas in which they were classified, but the statistics do provide a needed perspective on enrollment trends by the indicated subject matter areas.

The Size Leaders in Statistics

An aspect of the enrollment story that always had high appeal in the news media and to the reporting institutions is the size ranking of the top schools in full-time and grand total enrollments. It has been reiterated in the reports that size is neither a guarantee of, nor a substitute for, quality. Nevertheless, the rank order in enrollments does provide a means of measurement or quantification that is very visible and carries much weight in the assessment of higher education. In the years from 1919-20 through 1946-47, the 30 "representative" institutions always were ranked by size either in the main or supplementary enrollment articles. By 1921-22, in addition, Dr. Walters was listing the top 25 schools in size, irrespective of whether they were among the original 30 institutions. In 1961-62, the current author enlarged the list to include the top 30 institutions in full-time and grand total enrollments. A perusal of the tables over the 10 years of the 1960's reveals very clearly the pell-mell progress toward the creation of statewide or unitary college and university systems. This

---

sum of the separate full-time totals in the 1969-70 study is 4,144,499. The figure of 4,156,268, cited above and in the first paragraph of the 1969-70 study, includes figures for two institutions that reported too late for inclusion in the tables.

development has been especially important in California, New York, Wisconsin, Missouri, Texas, and North Carolina. In Ohio and many other states, state boards of regents or other similar bodies have been created to provide coordination and over-all direction of higher education in the state-supported institutions. This author has recognized the need for such administrative superstructure, but also has emphasized the need to maintain reasonable flexibility and diversity among the state institutions so that locally oriented strengths and innovative thrusts might be encouraged rather than stifled. Carbon copy colleges surely should not be the norm in a state system of higher education. On the other hand, reasonable statewide supervision can prevent needless and expensive duplication of effort, and can represent effectively the financial and other needs of higher education in the states. The rapid rise of the unitary state systems has affected the interpretation of the listing of the top 30 institutions by size. There is some disparity in comparing by size the California State Colleges as a system, or the State University of New York, for example, with a single-campus institution. It is a fact, however, that the state systems and the single-campus institutions coexist in the world of higher education, and the listing of the top 30 schools has recognized this situation. It is impractical to present a detailed analysis of the fluctuations in size over the 50-year period, even on a decennial basis. It is interesting, however, in Table III to compare the listing in 1919-20 of the 30 representative universities with the 1969-70 tabulation of the top 30 institutions in size order. This "before and after" sequence dramatically reveals some of the major developments in higher education in the last 50 years.

The Urban Aspects of Collegiate Enrollments

As early as 1920-21, Dr. Walters recognized the importance of enrollments, especially of part-time students, in the urban universities. The data in the tables disclosed "the extent to which the universities considered are cooperating in placing higher educational advantages within the reach of all who are qualified."[61] In many subsequent years, attention was given to urban university enrollments in both full-time and part-time categories. The normal practice was to cite enrollments for member institutions of the Associa-

---

[61] Raymond Walters, "Statistics of Registration of Thirty American Universities," *School & Society*, 13:378, Jan. 29, 1921, pp. 121-128.

tion of Urban Universities. Particular attention was given to this category in the 1960's. Their proximity to the great population masses of the country has placed the urban institutions in special positions of responsibility. Not only have they fulfilled the collegiate function of serving normal full-time students who may have been eligible and able to enroll elsewhere, but also that of providing educational opportunity for large numbers of commuting students for whom attendance in distant schools was impossible for financial or other reasons. In addition, the provision of general and continuing education curricula for adults, professionals, technicians, and the like has become increasingly important. Public service, especially in the local community, in all of its manifold capacities loomed especially large in the role of the urban schools in the later years. Indeed, with the mounting crisis conditions in the cities in the 1960's, the urban institutions were on the front line of community and social action as they increasingly assumed larger responsibilities in analyzing problems, proposing solutions, undertaking community service projects, and training personnel for community action posts. In many instances, the urban institutions bore the brunt of violence over issues of curriculum, civil rights, racism, poverty, and war. Whether they would or would not, they became deeply involved in community concerns. In 1967, Clark Kerr, writing as head of the Carnegie Corporation's Commission on the Future of Higher Education, suggested that the country needed "67 urban-grant universities to stand beside its 67 land-grant universities" to share responsibility for education, health, equal opportunity, and other vital concerns in urban areas. At the end of the 1960's, there was a continuing need for an identification between the urban institutions and their communities. The crisis of the cities presented perhaps the preeminent educational frontier of that time.[62] The 1939-40 report for 38 comparable urban universities showed 161,362 full-time and 320,732 grand total students—18.5% and 24.2%, respectively, of the total enrollments for the reporting and accredited institutions that year. By contrast, in 1969-70, there were 89 urban schools with 771,779 full-time and 1,213,177 grand total enrollees. The urban enrollments represented 19.4% of the full-time, 31.8% of

---

[62] Fred M. Hechinger, "A Call for the 'Urban-Grant' College," *The New York Times*, Oct. 22, 1967; Garland G. Parker, "Statistics of Attendance in American Universities and Colleges, 1967-68," *School & Society*, 96:2300, Jan. 6, 1968, p. 20.

the part-time, and 22.6% of the grand total students.[63] Any debate over the issue of involvement in community action and service by the urban institutions in the 1970's was merely academic; the questions were how much and in what ways they would be involved.

Matching of the Sexes

That enrollments involve animated and somewhat unpredictable human beings, and not just "dry-as-dust" data, is evidenced by an analysis of returns on the basis of sex. Even in the 1919-20 report on 30 universities, there were distinguishing figures for men and women in the tables and, in an increasingly sophisticated form, the tabulations by sex continued intermittently throughout the 50 years under review, and especially so in the 1960's. In general, the enrollment of women increased noticeably in prosperity periods, when jobs were plentiful, in wartime, and in the 1950's and 1960's. In 1959-60, men comprised 65% and women 35% of the reported full-time enrollments; by 1969-70, the respective percentages were 59.4% and 40.6%. The women always were ardent pursuants of the arts and sciences, teaching, nursing, and home economics curricula, but in the 1950's and 1960's they invaded historic male preserves in academia, particularly business administration and, to a lesser extent, engineering. The rising ratio of women to men in collegiate attendance has been advantageous to the country as well as to the women themselves in terms of good citizenship, child care, professional training, and cultural enrichment.

Collegians and the Geographical Spread

Higher education long has been marked by migratory tendencies as students have moved from one part of the country to another and from institution to institution as they pursued their academic goals. As referenced earlier, in 1934-35, a geographical table became a regular feature of the reports. In that year, the East North Central Region (Ohio, Indiana, Illinois, Michigan, and Wisconsin), with 136,777 comparably reported students, barely topped the Middle Atlantic Region (New York, New Jersey, and Pennsylvania), with

---

[63] Raymond Walters, "Statistics of Registration in American Universities and Colleges, 1939," *School & Society*, 50:1303, Dec. 16, 1939, pp. 769-788; Garland G. Parker, "Statistics of Attendance in American Universities and Colleges, 1969-70," *School & Society*, 98:2322, January, 1970, pp. 41-58.

135,086 students, to lead all sections in full-time enrollments.[64] In 1969-70, it is significant to record that the East North Central Region remained the leader, with 852,798 students, and the Middle Atlantic still ranked second, with 750,191 enrollees. Great growth in the 1950's and 1960's came in the Pacific, West South Central, and South Atlantic Regions, but the traditional strongholds of higher education in numbers still held their lead.[65]

Data on the Teachers

Frequent reference was made in the annual articles to the elusive nature of teacher statistics and their importance. Since the situation was set forth with some emphasis in the 1969-70 report, there is no need for reiteration here. It is suggested, however, that the parallel presentation of student and teacher numbers over 50 years in the reported categories provides source material for pedagogical research that is important. In Table IV, the citing of teacher data by decade gives a helpful overview of the half-century period.

GI's and Higher Education—"Operation Veterans"

Emphasis was given earlier to higher education for veterans in the post-World War II and post-Korean war periods. The aim here is to complete a survey of the 25-year story of what might be termed "Operation Veterans." The initial basis of the legal code covering education for veterans was the Servicemen's Readjustment Act of 1944 (Public Law 78-346) that provided for direct payments to the institution to cover a veteran's tuition, fees, and laboratory, library, and other normal school costs, for up to $500 per year. Also, there was a monthly subsistence allowance for full-time students—initially $50 for single veterans and $75 for those with dependents, but adjusted in 1945 to $75 and $120, respectively. Veterans not dishonorably discharged and with 90 days or more of service after Sept. 16, 1940, and through July 26, 1947, as later determined, were eligible for educational benefits. They were entitled to one year of full-time training plus a period equal to their time in service, up to 48 months, and the termination date was July 25, 1956. There were 2,230,000

[64] Raymond Walters, "Statistics of Registration in American Universities and Colleges, 1934," *School & Society*, 40:1042, Dec. 15, 1934, p. 8.

[65] Garland G. Parker, "Statistics of Attendance in American Universities and Colleges, 1969-70," *School & Society*, 98:2322, January, 1970, p. 54.

veterans who received educational benefits at the college level under this legislation.

For Korean Conflict veterans, the Veterans Readjustment Assistance Act of 1952 (PL 82-550) was enacted providing direct payment of $110 a month to veterans with no dependents who were full-time students. The subsidy increased to $135 with one dependent and to $160 when there were additional dependents. No payments were made to the veterans for tuition, books, supplies, and other costs. Those who had served 90 or more days without dishonorable discharges after June 27, 1950, and before Feb. 1, 1955, as later determined, could claim educational benefits for a period equal to one-and-one-half times the duration of their active service, up to a maximum of 36 months. The termination date was Jan. 31, 1965, and a total of 1,213,000 veterans were trained at the college level under this law.

The Veterans Readjustment Benefits Act of 1966 (PL 89-358), then referred to as the Cold War GI Bill, provided for post-Korean veterans. At first, it set direct payments to veterans with no dependents at $100 a month, at $125 with one dependent, and at $150 with more than one dependent; in 1967, the respective rates were raised to $130, $155, and $175, with an additional $10 for each dependent over two. Veterans with other than dishonorable discharges and more than 180 service days, any portion of which was subsequent to Jan. 31, 1955, were entitled to one month of education for each month of service, with a maximum of 36 months. On Dec. 1, 1968, this was changed to allow entitlement to one and one-half months for each month of service, and, if there were 18 months or more of service after Jan. 31, 1955, a full 36 months, provided the veteran had completed his military obligation. To claim benefits, the eligible veteran was required to complete his education and training by May 31, 1974, or within eight years after separation from service, whichever came later. By the end of the 1968-69 academic year, some 701,200 post-Korean veterans had claimed educational benefits in institutions of higher learning. Thus, by June 22, 1969, the 25th anniversary of the original GI Bill, well over 4,000,000 veterans had received some college-level training under Public Laws 346, 550, and 358.[66]

---

[66] *25th Anniversary of the GI Bill: Fact Sheet for Editors, Broadcasters, Writers* (Veterans Administration Information Service, Washington, D.C., 1969), pp. 1-11.

In addition to the above acts, there were other significant, but smaller, service-related benefit programs for disabled veterans, as well as for orphans and widows of veterans. Annual reference was made in the collegiate enrollment reports to developments relating to veterans' education. Veterans' enrollments steadily declined in the first half of the 1960's. The ending of PL 346, it was noted in 1965-66, lowered the curtain on one of the most significant educational acts in history. The enrollment of veterans and war orphans, as of Oct. 31, 1965, was only 20,963—the low point of the decade. By 1966-67, however, veteran enrollments again were increasing as a result of the passage of PL 358 for post-Korean veterans; the total of 206,804 on Oct. 31, 1966, was an 89% increase over the previous year. The law was amended in favor of the veterans in 1967, and came to be known as the Vietnam or Post-Korean Era GI Bill. On Oct. 31, 1969, the Veterans Administration reported 367,266 collegiate enrollees to close out the 1960's with the highest count for the decade.[67]

Without question, the 25-year saga of support for veterans comprises one of the most significant success stories in the history of higher education. The observation in the 1965-66 report, subsequent to the expiration of PL 346, that the bill had helped "service men and women by the millions to exchange their guns for sheepskins to the inestimable betterment not only of themselves but the whole of society" is valid for the other aid measures as well. The merging of millions of men who, on the average, had been away for 30 months into the mainstream of post-World War II American life was facilitated greatly by the educational benefits of the GI Bill, and, possibly, it helped to stave off serious disruption of American economic life.

The influence of the veterans upon the ebb and flow of academic life was important. Significant curricular and calendar changes resulted, and the presence of these older and more mature students in the classrooms imparted an aura of seriousness and urgency in higher education that was unusual. The fact that so many veterans were married and brought their families onto campus or into neighboring

---

[67] Garland G. Parker, "Statistics of Attendance in American Universities and Colleges, 1965-66," *School & Society*, 94:2270, Jan. 8, 1966, pp. 20-21; "Statistics of Attendance . . . , 1966-67," *School & Society*, 95:2285, Jan. 7, 1967, p. 24; "Statistics of Attendance . . . , 1967-68," *School & Society*, 96:2300, Jan. 6, 1968, p. 23; "Statistics of Attendance . . . , 1969-70," *School & Society*, 98:2322, January, 1970, pp. 57-58.

areas had an important impact upon social life and living arrangements for all students. Adult and continuing education programs
were stimulated greatly by the needs of veterans, and were reflected
in programs of most institutions many years later. The greatest
gains, of course, went to the veterans themselves, who profited not
only economically and professionally, but whose lives were enriched
by the educational experiences often made possible only by the GI
Bill of Rights. On a cash basis, hindsight suggests that the nation
made one of its best investments in supporting the GI Bill Education and Training Program. The Veterans Administration estimates
that the average veteran eventually will repay in additional taxes, on
an income larger than he otherwise would have earned, a sum that
is several times the cost of his VA educational benefits.[68] In the
1969-70 report, the author discussed some considerations of concern
pertaining to the ongoing support of higher education for veterans,
and concluded that there was high need for continued attention to
this important enterprise. Special attention was being given to the
needs of military service personnel prior to their discharge at the
close of the 1960's via the Transition Program under joint sponsorship
of the Department of Defense and the U.S. Office of Education.
This program was directed particularly at military servicemen who
had derived from disadvantaged population groups and who generally had been unmotivated and often were unqualified for college
admissions. Special techniques were developed for counseling and
training prior to their discharge and for providing information of
collegiate opportunities and support programs that might be available for them. This was an aggressive and constructive aid program
that offered much promise of success.[69]

The Junior Colleges—50 Years of Growth

One of the most dynamic developments in higher education, especially in the 1950's and 1960's, has been that associated with junior
colleges. These units also are referred to as private, public, independent, comprehensive, technical, vocational, two-year, and community
colleges. The scope of this account precludes a detailed historical

---

[68] *GI Bill of Rights 25th Anniversary Fact Sheet*, pp. 11, 18.

[69] *Transition Program: How to MOVE UP through Higher Education* (Washington, D.C.: Office of the Assistant Secretary of Defense, Manpower and
Reserve Affairs, November, 1969), pp. 1-314.

treatment, but it is helpful to recall that the 1835-1900 period was important for the evolution of private junior colleges in the U.S., and the years 1901-20 marked the early development of the two-year public colleges. In 1920, 8,000 students were enrolled in 52 junior colleges across 23 states; by 1921-22, there were 16,000 students in 207 junior colleges, of which 70 were public and 137 private. A revealing junior colleges study by Kelly and Wilbur in 1969 showed that by 1947 the private colleges had reached their largest number with 323, but that public junior colleges surpassed them in 1952 with a total of 327.[70]

Before 1921, the junior college academic emphasis was on courses that could be transferred to a four-year college or university, and the concept of an associate in arts degree slowly emerged. Between 1921 and 1947, the emphasis shifted to technical and vocational programs that were labeled "terminal," and the number of all two-year institutions rose to about 560 in 1941, with some 200,000 students enrolled. In the period after 1948, the great thrust was toward development of comprehensive community colleges, with New York and California as state pacesetters in the junior college field. The programs of the junior colleges after World War II especially were suited for those veterans who sought two-year terminal programs that were technical-vocational in nature; this demand contributed to the growth of the comprehensive community colleges.[71]

The American Association of Junior Colleges was established in 1920, and in recent decades the executive officers of that body often have provided the authors of the *School & Society* enrollment reports with enrollment information on the two-year schools. The first Walters' comment on junior college enrollments was in 1931-32, when it was suggested that enrollment in some state universities and private colleges might have been held down because of the attendance of many students in their home junior colleges.[72] In 1932-33, attention was called to the rapid growth of junior college enrollments in Michigan and Kansas. In that year, there were 106,016 students in 497 colleges; in 1933-34, the numbers were 105,457 students in 519

---

[70] Win Kelly and Leslie Wilbur, "Junior College Development in the United States," *School & Society*, 97:2321, December, 1969, pp. 485-498, 520.

[71] *Ibid.*, pp. 488-490.

[72] Raymond Walters, "Statistics of Registration in American Universities and Colleges, 1931," *School & Society*, 34:885, Dec. 12, 1931, p. 784.

junior colleges.[73] By 1939-40, there were 575 schools, with 196,710 students. The number had climbed to 634 junior colleges and 562,786 students in 1949-50; of these, 329 were public, with 456,291 students, and 305 were private junior colleges, with 106,495 enrollees. Enrollments continued to grow and colleges to increase in the 1950's, but the decade of the 1960's was the boom period for junior colleges. In 1959-60, junior college enrollments approximated 640,-500; by 1968-69, the count was 1,945,116. It appeared likely that the number in 1969-70 would approach 2,250,000 students.[74] Precise figures are elusive in the junior college field, but there were about 720 junior colleges in 1964-65, and 993 were reported for October, 1968, in the *Junior College Directory,* by the American Association of Junior Colleges. This number included 254 private and 739 public junior colleges, of which 97 had enrollments of 5,000 or more.[75] By 1969-70, there were approximately 1,060 junior colleges in the country.

Throughout the 1960's, the author gave increasing emphasis to enrollments and academic considerations involving the junior colleges. The rapid rise of these colleges had important implications for the four-year schools. It meant a great increase in transfer students at the upper-division level, and larger classes in the junior and senior groups. Matters such as accreditation of the two-year schools, curricular correlation between the two- and four-year units, advanced standing, admissions requirements for transfer students, and academic and administrative articulation between the two school groups became increasingly important.[76] To their great advantage, many of the hundreds of recently founded junior colleges generally were unfettered by the traditions, statutes, and academic bureaucracy that so often impede educational progress. The result was that many of the most innovative, exciting, and productive educational enterprises of the decade transpired on the two-year campuses. New frontiers were probed in academic programs, technical and vocational programs, teaching techniques, teacher recruitment, and community service. Lower-division enrollments began to stabilize in some institu-

---

[73] Raymond Walters, "Statistics of Registration in American Universities and Colleges, 1934," *School & Society,* 40:1042, Dec. 15, 1934, p. 787.
[74] Garland G. Parker, "A Supplementary Report on Collegiate Enrollments for 1968-69," *School & Society,* 98:2323, February, 1969, p. 118.
[75] Kelly and Wilbur, *op. cit.,* p. 490.
[76] Garland G. Parker, "A Supplementary Report on Collegiate Enrollments for 1966-67," *School & Society,* 95:2288, Feb. 18, 1967, p. 125.

tions and, in the long run, might decline or even disappear. Some senior colleges with enrollments limited to the upper two years and graduate programs appeared on the educational scene. The junior college network became so extended that most students in the nation could find collegiate education available at moderate cost within 50 miles or less from their homes. By 1975, it was anticipated that there might be 1,500 junior colleges enrolling 50% or more of all freshmen and perhaps a total of 3,000,000 or more students.[77] The anticipated posture of the two-year colleges in the 1970's was set forth succinctly in November, 1969, by Leo A. Munday, as follows: "Under the pressure of current social trends in America, universal post-secondary education arises as a possible national objective for the 1970's. Several social trends appear to coalesce around this idea. Jobs are becoming more complex and are requiring higher levels of skills. More trained personnel will be needed in technical and service fields. And there is widespread concern about providing greater access to economic opportunity for the country's minorities.

"Among institutions of higher education, the two-year colleges are the most likely ones for many Americans to accomplish this education. Founded on a spirit of egalitarianism these 'open door' institutions generally emphasize a broad curriculum which includes many fields geared to specific occupational requirements."[78] Truly, a dramatic and democratizing new dimension had been added to American higher education by the rapid rise of the comprehensive junior colleges and related schools. The social and economic, as well as the educational, implications were significant, and would deserve high priority attention in the years ahead.

---

[77] Garland G. Parker, "A Supplementary Report on Collegiate Enrollments for 1968-69," *School & Society*, 98:2323, February, 1969, p. 118.

[78] *The Two-Year College and Its Students: An Empirical Report*, Monograph Two (Iowa City, Iowa: American College Testing Program, 1969), p. vii.

7. Crossing Points into the 1970's

As the nation emerged from the 1960's and searched for its future in the 1970's, many problems interposed themselves as decennial crossing points. Some were of special concern in higher education and merit brief attention here.

Inflation, Finance, and Taxes

A galloping inflation that raced ahead at a near-six per cent annual rate in 1969 constituted a financial hazard that threatened to extend into the 1970's. Taxpayer revolts at the ballot box resulted in a rising rate of tax levy and bond issue rejections as the people struck out at one of the few public targets directly available to them—ironically, their own local school systems. After a decade of ever-rising appropriations, state legislatures were taking a long look at requests for further increases from state-assisted institutions. A presidential veto in January, 1970, of a bulging appropriations bill for the Department of Health, Education, and Welfare signaled a possible slowdown in the level, or at least the rate of increase, of Federal spending in support of higher education. The private schools were hard-pressed and seeking even more diligently for aid from the public sector. In short, leaner budget years perhaps lay ahead, and would have to be taken into account in institutional financial planning for the 1970's.

Quality of the Environment

Quite belatedly, but hopefully not too late, private and public enterprise began to focus upon a national crusade against the pollution of air, water, and the total environment. The first official act of 1970 by Pres. Nixon was the signing of a bill to create a Council on Environment Quality to operate within the Presidential office and lead a massive attack on pollution problems.[79] In view of the intertwining technical, social, economic, and political issues in this campaign, it was clear that colleges and universities should, and would, be deeply involved. Fortunately, some institutions—such as the University of Cincinnati with its Institute of Environmental Health—had pioneered in this field many years before. Even so, all of the expertise the nation could muster on its college campuses would be needed in an all-out struggle against smog and the desecration of water and land resources so vital to the existence of the nation and its people.

Population Problems

Awareness of an impending population crisis exploded with the figurative impact of an atomic bomb around the turn of the decade of the 1970's. A procreative process that had produced 1,000,000,000 living people by 1850, 2,000,000,000 by 1930, perhaps 3,500,000,000 by 1970, and might yield 7,000,000,000 in another 30 years was a force that must be taken into account on an earth whose space and resources obviously are limited. In the U.S., a populace that numbered 204,000,000 in 1969 gave promise of rising to 300,000,000 by the year 2000. Earlier birthrate figures were such that collegiate enrollments probably would rise only at moderate rates in the 1970's, and even might hit a plateau in the early 1980's, but thereafter the likelihood of ponderous increases again would be great. The personal, emotional, religious, and political issues involved in population control indicate the sensitive nature of an issue to which higher education perforce would address itself in the 1970's. Given the

---

[79] *The Cincinnati Enquirer,* Jan. 2, 1970.

propensities of biological engineering suggested by genetic research in the late 1960's, the complexity of this delicate problem became all the more obvious.

The Poverty Line

Despite all laudable progress in the 1960's, the fact remained that some 25,000,000 Americans still remained at or near the poverty level by the end of the decade. By common consent, this was too many, but the programs for reducing the number were a subject of great debate. Negative income tax arrangements, a Federal support program for every family up to a designated dollar minimum, and work incentive policies were among the approaches under consideration. The nation probably would have to recognize that, in its large and increasing population, there always would be many millions who were the deserving needy and another uncertain element that would qualify for aid although undeserving. No less an authority than John W. Gardner, chairman of the Urban Coalition Action Council and former Secretary of Health, Education, and Welfare, testified before Congress in January, 1970, that there probably were no more than 1,100,000 persons on welfare who could be regarded as likely candidates for gainful employment.[80] In the long run, the best answer to the welfare problem for the latter group undoubtedly lay in an effective and constructive program of education that would instill incentive, stimulate motivation, and provide training and skills that would enable more of the poor to join the nation's labor force. This would require a heavy expenditure of energy, ingenuity, and resources by the colleges and universities working in unison with social, state, and Federal agencies as well as with business and industry. Success in this area probably would offer much promise for securing the public welfare, supporting private enterprise, and maintaining representative government.

The Issue of Race

Perhaps the most critical crossing point of all was the tenuous structure that bridged relations between the races. In the 1960's, the American people, by and large, recognized the racial problem for what it was, and began a serious search for solutions. Understanda-

---

[80] *The Cincinnati Post & Times-Star,* Jan. 26, 1970.

bly, but regrettably, the achievements of the 1960's, though significant, were minimal in comparison to the larger challenge that lay
ahead for the 1970's. Equality of opportunity, sometimes priority of
position for the future, and even reparation for past disadvantages
were oft-presented demands of the black minority. The legal
obstacles impeding improved relations among races had been re-
moved, but traditional barriers of emotion, psychology, prejudice,
and economics remained. Whether or not the black and white popu-
lations would share the blessings and burdens of American life
together in an increasingly integrated pattern or would withdraw by
mutual consent into islands of segregation and separatism as yet was
unresolved. The great search of the 1970's undoubtedly will be
concerned with the promotion of better relations among all races.
Education is no panacea for social ills, but higher education would
have a role of inestimable importance in seeking solutions to racial
problems in the new decade and those to follow. Efforts in this area
would be reflected in innovative approaches and serious attention to
recruitment, admissions, curricular reforms, personnel practices, and
community service. There was hope, at least, that the cooperative
efforts of the various ethnic groups would result in a racial accom-
modation that would grant to all persons reasonable chances for
success and the pursuit of happiness. Alternative possibilities—such
as accelerated separatism, continued civil disobedience, increasing
hostility, rising violence, and even guerrilla warfare—were not pleas-
ant to contemplate, and emphasized the desperate need for determined efforts by all groups to find tolerable answers to the perplexing
problems of race.

Crisis in the Cities and Crime

A certainty of the 1970's was that urban problems would demand
high attention. The creation in the 1960's of the Department of
Housing and Urban Development dramatized the importance of the
crisis in the cities. Out-migration of affluent whites and blacks, the
infusion of low-income groups and welfare clients, increasing tax
burdens, and growing technical complexities of life and society generally in the megalopolis pointed up the particular problems of the
inner city. Sanitation, garbage and waste disposal, air and water
pollution, traffic congestion, insufficient park areas, and blackboard
jungle conditions in many schools added to the handicaps of the

cities. High interest rates, construction declines, deteriorating buildings, increasing rents, and spiraling inflation were factors in 1970 that
impeded desperately needed improvements in urban housing. Finally, these circumstances, in concert with the spill-over influences of
a breakdown in family life, a decline in societal and personal
discipline, and the disorder deriving from racial disputes, created an
inner-city environment especially conducive to crime. Life in the
inner cities—especially in the larger ones and particularly in Washington, D.C.—was unsafe, and crime was rampant. Crime control
would levy heavily upon the combined resources of the cities, the
states, and the nation, and would depend upon the sympathetic support
of the people. Beyond all this, however, there were new frontiers of
human, social, and city engineering that needed to be explored. The
cross-contributions of sociologists, social workers, police forces, engineers, architects, and scientists in many fields would be needed.
Interdisciplinary approaches to the solution of city problems would
require maximum contributions from colleges and universities in
research and community service. Already, many institutions had
created departments or schools of city or community planning that
endeavored to muster the personnel and resources needed for a
broad frontal attack on urban problems. Even more massive efforts
would be required as the nation sought to determine whether or not
its people could look forward to a free and safe society in megalopolis, or whether they faced the necessity of retreating into a fortress-
like security system to protect life and property. Few challenges
rang louder on the cymbal of the 1970's as Americans listened for the
lead in the hectic tempo of the times. Colleges and universities,
especially the urban ones, could look forward to deep involvement in
the battle for the cities and against crime.

Dissent and Consent

Another unresolved issue ushered into the 1970's was how to
tolerate minority dissent to the maximum extent possible and yet
maintain the rights and the freedoms owed to the majority. The
dividing lines between the perimeters of toleration and the ramparts
of intolerance are difficult to distinguish, but the search for them
must be never-ceasing on the part of a people that strives for a free
society. Generally speaking, the American people, by common consent, have agreed upon the goals to be set and the latitude allowed

its governing agents in the different eras of our history. In some periods, such as 1861-65, this consent dissolved, and surely it was shaken in the 1960's. In the 1970's, a high priority goal should be finding a formula that would allow reasonable dissent, and yet comprehend the common consent that is essential to the successful functioning of this society. Social scientists and other university-level experts, civic groups, government leaders, and all citizens will need to devote an unprecedented energy to this fateful enterprise, for failure well might mean chaos and the end of the system under which the nation has operated for almost 200 years.

The Restive Young

The alienation of sizable segments of young Americans from the "silent majority" or the "establishment" remained a serious concern for the 1970's. Whether or not the restive young—after emerging from the limbo of an extended adolescent-like existence that was in part the result of a prolonged education time span—would rejoin the mainstream of American society was not resolved. If they did not, the resulting state of schism would have unfortunate consequences for society as a whole. If eventually they did join the establishment, take jobs, and assume normal responsibilities, it was likely that their long-term influence would be used within the system to implement the ideas they had espoused so vigorously, and sometimes violently, in their youth. Under any circumstances, never again would there be a reversion to the mores of former decades. The likelihood was that the legal trappings of adulthood would be affixed to youth at age 18 rather than 21, not only in respect to voting and military service, but also in areas such as sexual freedom, housing, contractual obligations, and property rights. Student opinion no doubt would support demands for continued and extended participation in campus governance and curricular change. There was little reason to think that ethnic minorities would not continue to demand additional reforms favorable to their particular interests. Administrations, faculties, and government authorities seemed prepared to exercise more effective control over campus disorders than in the late 1960's, but it was unlikely that dissident groups would cease and desist in their efforts either to change or to overthrow the established order in higher education. By its historic insistence upon freedom of dissent, toleration of difference, and resistance to outside authority, the university community is most vulnerable to activist or violent groups that seek to impose their will in utter disregard of the normal academic process. Those who press unreasonably for their pet projects best had be thoughtful of the price they may exact for their gains. Beyond a yet undefined pressure limit, it was likely that the authorities would use force to counter force, and the death of the free university as previously known could be the result. There is precedent for such sequence in the events of history. At any rate, students, faculties, administrations, and directive boards would be well-advised to exercise constructive leadership, reasonable restraint, and responsible authority as they sought the betterment of higher education in the 1970's.

Higher Education at the Crossroads

There were crossing points peculiar to higher education as the nation moved into the 1970's. Problems of finance and student unrest were alluded to earlier. The conflict of interest between teaching and research was unresolved yet. Students were expected to continue their demand for college teaching to be more effective and for better rapport between professor and student. The students still asked for curricular "relevance" to life situations as they saw them. This countered the traditional intellectual view that all knowledge is generally relevant, and that standards of relevance vary with age groups and with the changing social scene. A clash between the mature scholar and the student apprentice on the subject of relevance undoubtedly would be a continuing controversy. A search for new teaching techniques hopefully would be pursued in the 1970's. Innovations might include more emphasis on independent study, foreign study, team teaching, programmed learning, community service, educational television, work-study plans, residence hall-centered learning experiences, honors programs, more interdisciplinary programs, and many other as yet undefined approaches to learning improvement. The growth of junior colleges, university branches, and academic centers; the expansion of technical-vocational education programs; and the balance that should prevail between graduate and undergraduate programs all were considerations that would demand attention in the 1970's.[81] Open or selective admissions, the extension of tutorial and remedial service, the

[81] *The Chronicle of Higher Education*, Dec. 8, 1969.

advantage to be bequeathed to the disadvantaged, and the feasible level of financial aid to be supplied to needy and/or academically able students were other issues for continued consideration. Pronouncements from the U.S. Office of Education in late 1969 indicated that education at all levels would face demands for quantification of student and teacher performance. That is, measureable results would be demanded in return for financial subsidy in defined areas. It was anticipated that the doctrine of "accountability" would replace "relevance" as the key word in higher education.[82] Planned programmed budgeting for institutions and state systems promised to quantify all educational endeavor and even to question the validity of continuing appropriations. Higher education apparently was headed for an era of "taut ship" operations, in which all activities and expenditures would be subject to critical and continuous review.

The Violent Spring of 1970

The invasion of Cambodia by U.S. and South Vietnamese forces on May 1, 1970, resulted in demonstrations and protests that exploded into violence on dozens of college and university campuses across the nation. Tragic episodes involving the death of several students at Kent State University in Ohio and Jackson State College in Mississippi brought shock to a distraught nation and its millions of college students. The Cambodian, Kent State, and Jackson State issues, provocative as they were, however, only provided the precipitating factors for the student unrest, activism, and violence of the sad spring of 1970. Many of the basic and more deeply rooted factors are those covered in this study of 50 years of development in the nation, society, and higher education. The fateful events of 1970 added even more significance to the nation's search for solutions to its grave problems in the years ahead.

Focus on the Future

The intent has been to emphasize both negative and positive factors in this analysis of the state of the nation and higher education. No law of progress guarantees the success or survival of this or any nation; history attests amply to this assertion. Whether or not we survive and prosper depends largely upon our wise use of the

---

[82] *Higher Education and National Affairs*, Dec. 5, 1969, p. 7.

human talent and physical resources in this great land. Whether or not we will exercise the necessary judgment and social discipline to assure all men and all groups that they have a chance to share in the great American dream is as yet uncertain. This writer agrees with Max Lerner and others that it still is possible that the dream can be shared and realized by all segments of the American people—just possible! The extent to which this can be done will depend in great measure on how responsibly and effectively higher education performs its various functions in our society.

 **APPENDIX**

Statistics of Attendance
in American Universities
and Colleges, 1969-70

*The following report on collegiate enrollments for 1969-70 original-
ly appeared in* School & Society, January, 1970. *As the 50th article in
the series of annual reports in* School & Society, *and as a national
study of an eventful year in the history of higher education and the
U.S., it is being included in this book. The 1969-70 report reflects
in fact and interpretation many of the challenges and changes in
the dynamic decade of the 1960's and provides a documentary as
well as a literary base for a consideration of the crossover into the
crucial 1970's. Since the decade of the 1970's may prove to be either
a pathway of decline or a high road to new peaks of progress, the
50th* School & Society *enrollment report takes on added significance
as a study base for an analysis of our educational and national prob-*

lems. In addition to its contemporary reference value, the report is included as an illustration of the tabular, statistical, and interpretive methodology that developed in the first 50 years of the report series.

THIS SURVEY of 1969-70 includes 1,145 accredited institutions in the U.S. and Puerto Rico. It covers accredited universities, senior colleges, four-year colleges, and two-year schools administered by institutions in the first three categories.[83] In all reporting schools, there were 4,156,268 full-time students and a grand total of 5,744,335. The twofold purpose is to tabulate and interpret the enrollments and other data reported by these selected institutions. Tables 1-6 present the basic data; here the aim is to give the figures substance and meaning.

Freshman Enrollment Swell Continues

Consistent with population trends and an increase of 4.9% in 1968-69, freshman students in the autumn of 1969 numbered 922,111 in 948 comparably reporting institutions, a gain of 4.5%. With an estimated increase in 18-year-olds of only 2.88% in 1969-70, the

---

[83] DEFINITIONS. The official definitions underlying the report this year, essentially the same as those used for the last 10 years, are listed below:

The *full-time student* devotes substantially all of his working or study time to his college curriculum. This is interpreted generally to mean 12 degree-credit hours, presumably 75% of a normal load or more, but may be less for graduate students. The presumption is that students so classified would pay full-time tuition and fees. The *part-time student* normally takes courses, that may be counted toward a degree, in the late afternoon, on Saturday, in the evening, frequently in the day, or by extension, and enrolls for fewer than 12 credits, or less than 75% of a normal load.

The *full-time teaching staff* is composed of those persons holding rank of instructor or equivalent and higher rank in full-time employment for the academic year who give at least half their time to instruction. The *total teaching staff* includes *both* full-time teaching staff and part-time individuals, including lecturers, fellows, teaching assistants; research assistants, if they teach; and others who teach.

Freshmen are presumed to be full-time persons classified as first-year or freshman undergraduate students. They are not necessarily first-time, degree-credit students, because such a restriction would preclude the listing of any students now registered as freshmen who began their college work in the previous winter, spring, or summer, after the last annual report was published.

Unless otherwise designated, as in the above paragraph, it is presumed that all degree-credit students at all levels (undergraduate, graduate, and professional) will be counted in the various categories.

college attending rate of this age group still appears to be rising.[84]

It is regrettable that many large and prestigious institutions of the nation apparently were incapable of reporting their freshman enrollments by Nov. 15, 1969, when it was mandatory to close the comparability tables. The oft-repeated alibi for nonreporting is computer troubles. Few have been more critical than this writer of the often frustrating and inadequate performance in the whirring world of computers and, at the same time, more thankful for the reporting miracles that electronic data processing makes possible. It is lamentable to note that 10 years ago freshman data were readily available in most schools by Oct. 15, but that, in 1969, it frequently was not ready by November or even December 15. As one who himself has had extensive exposure to computerization in an institution enrolling over 35,000 students, the author, in all fairness, has to express his conviction that some reporting officers use computer problems as shields for slow or nonperformance on their part. He has little sympathy for those officers who either resist or resent the supplying of enrollment data for this or other legitimate enrollment reports. Higher education is an enterprise of prime importance to the nation as well as to our institutions, and the desire should be to share, rather than restrict, enrollment information. Fortunately, that is the view and policy of the overwhelming majority of reporting officers, and to them this writer expresses his appreciation and that of a grateful nation.

The data for the reporting schools support the author's earlier estimate that the number of freshmen will approach or surpass 1,000,000 in the four-year accredited schools, inclusive of their affiliated two-year units, and that there are about 2,000,000 new freshmen in all of the nation's some 2,500 higher education institutions.[85] The latter figure comprehends both full-time and part-time students in degree- and nondegree-credit programs.

Their role as harbingers of future total enrollments and the implications they have for the nation's pool of trained manpower lend high significance to full-time freshman enrollments. As noted in 1968-69, despite the dissent that confuses the picture of higher education today, ever-increasing numbers of collegians pursue edu-

---

[84] *Projections of Educational Statistics to 1976-77* (1967 Edition, U.S. Office of Education, Washington, D.C.: U.S. Government Printing Office, 1968), p. 110.

[85] Press release, University of Cincinnati Public Information Office, Oct. 29, 1969.

cational objectives. Continued emphasis upon the recruitment of the disadvantaged among both whites and blacks, financial assistance, reliance upon collegiate attendance as partial military draft protection, social and economic stimuli, the rising need for expertise and trained leadership in the operation of our increasingly complex and technical society, and the affluence of so many citizens help explain the continued rise in enrollments. Population data and other factors suggest that freshman increases through 1979 will be comparable to those in the last two years.[86] Even though sharp percentage increases will be unlikely in any given year, the large enrollment base will mean an increase in total numbers each year that must be labeled as massive. Throughout the decade of the 1970's, therefore, the nation and its higher education system will be called upon to serve a steadily increasing student body, and appropriate planning to that end deserves high national and institutional priority.

For many years, it has been the practice in these annual reports to survey freshman enrollments in the selected fields of arts and sciences, engineering, business administration, agriculture, education, nursing, and a miscellaneous or "all others" category. This classification perhaps was more meaningful in former years than in 1969-70. In reflection of the increasing popularity of core curriculum requirements for all freshmen in the first two years of college and the trend toward a general college organization in many universities, the data for classified freshmen have declined in validity. An increasing number and proportion of freshmen have been reported in the arts and sciences and the "all others" categories. Since determination of program majors within the collegiate framework of most universities is a secondary computer programming chore, many institutions contend that enrollment data for freshmen by the required areas can not be made available in time for this report. To the extent that this is so, it is another reflection of the increasingly complex reporting structure in higher education that interposes an additional obstacle to the securing of needed data for valid academic planning and budgeting. Despite this data deterioration, the fact remains that this annual survey is the only one that has provided national figures by program area at the freshman level over a period of many years. Further-

---

[86] The estimated percentage increases in 18-year-olds from 1969 through 1979 are as follows: 2.88, 2.94, 3.39, 2.17, 2.15, 1.16, 2.15, .46, .36, .86, and 1.93. Thereafter, through 1985, there are estimated percentage declines each year as follows: 1.93, 1.91, .66, 2.7, 4.68, 3.86, and .13. *Projections of Educational Statistics to 1976-77, loc. cit.*

more, the results remain informative and indicative of trends in the subject matter fields reviewed. It is justifiable, therefore, in this 50th report, to survey the statistics by category and offer some interpretation of them.

Nursing Majors Show Highest Percentage Rise—7.5%

For the first time since nursing students began to be reported here in 1961-62, freshmen in this vital field numbered 14,601 in degree programs and led the other subject matter groups with a 7.5% increase. Of the total, 266 were men and 14,335 were women. This increase only partially meets the critical need in this profession. Anyone who recently has been a patient or visitor in, or has had a professional relationship with, a hospital must be aware of the desperate shortage of trained nurses that perplexes most healing arts institutions.

Education Students Still Hold a High Percentage Place

A frequent front runner, the education freshmen were second only to the nurses, with a percentage increase of 5.2%. A total of 111,568 freshmen were reported as potential education majors, but the actual number was larger because of the extent to which they were hidden in general college counts. When we are mindful of the mushrooming of problems in our schools—such as ghettoization, busing and other integration controversies, the rising rate of physical attacks upon teachers, curricular disputes, administrator-teacher hassles, encroaching unionism, looming financial problems, and the discontent of the taxpayer—it is surprising, but encouraging, that so many young people elect teaching as a career. Budding young teachers would be well-advised, however, to survey the teaching field opportunities carefully before electing a major. The fact that so many choose social studies as a preferred teacher training curriculum may be dramatic testimony to their interest in the social ills of the nation, but it also may reflect a desire to avoid the higher mathematics and science course content that characterizes other curricula. With perhaps no more than one teacher placement available each year for every five or six baccalaureate-trained new social studies teachers in our schools, these young people should be forewarned of their chances for employment. No doubt it is true that the training these young people receive in such programs prepares them for other vocations, but they nonetheless may be pre-empting spaces in our teacher training programs that better could be used for preparation of specialists in other fields where the need is more critical.

Agriculture Freshmen Third in Percentage Rise— 4.4%

Freshmen labeled as agriculture majors, consistent with a trend that traces back to 1964, show an increase of 4.4% for 1969-70, with 14,339 tabulated in degree programs. The forecasts of the current crop of gloomy neo-Malthusian prognosticators are not calculated to set our minds at ease, when we are mindful of the population deluge that is prophesied and the perhaps hopeless task of feeding the multiplying millions in the decades ahead. Undoubtedly, the country, and indeed the world, will need all of the trained agriculturists and their colleagues in other compatible scientific disciplines that can be recruited for the battle of the food line that looms up ahead.

Arts and Sciences Next in the Freshman Hierarchy—Up by 4%

Always a leader in the freshman gain groups, those students entering arts and sciences programs in the comparable schools in 1969-70 numbered 450,834 and increased by four per cent, a bit shy of their 4.3% rise in 1968-69. While it is clear that this group comprehends many who later will elect professional career programs, it is significant that so many collegians have so much exposure to the arts and sciences. As trumpeted annually in this paragraph, the author contends that the close acquaintance of a large segment of our citizenry with the great minds, great books, and great ideas of the ages is essential to the successful functioning of a representative democracy. Indeed, it is asserted that the tendency among too many people today to disdain and even ignore the knowledge and lessons of the past is not unrelated to the eruption of violence among the dissidents of the present. We need the accumulated knowledge and experience of yesterday as well as the innovative and creative genius

(Text continued on page 135)

TABLE 1

I. UNIVERSITIES AND LARGE INSTITUTIONS OF COMPLEX ORGANIZATION

1. Under Public Control

Institution	Men Full-time	Women Full-time	Grand Total Students	Full-time Teaching Staff	Total Teaching Staff
Arizona State U. —	10,760	6,745	27,468	900	1,330
Auburn U.	8,733	4,343	15,115	720	910
Bowling Green State U.	6,913	6,444	15,559	692	1,117
Central Michigan U.	5,358	6,088	14,983	503	662
City University of New York, including	(37,954)	(35,053)	(167,302)	(5,192)	(10,558)
Brooklyn C.	5,964	6,147	24,768	914	1,630
City C.	7,986	4,317	20,153	777	1,426
Hunter C.	1,587	5,181	18,334	619	1,173
Queens C.	5,826	7,100	23,355	619	1,424
Bernard M. Baruch C.	2,328	611	10,003	246	704
Herbert H. Lehman C.	11,595	10,081	47,654	1,351	1,910
Richmond C.	719	482	14,641	257	487
York C.	643	589	2,299	83	137
University Division of Graduate Studies			1,250	97	124
John Jay C. of Criminal Justice	718	482	1,677	65	65
6 Community Colleges	475	40	3,032	70	99
Mt. Sinai School of Medicine	113	23	136	94	1,379
Colorado State U.	8,956	5,375	16,252	746	1,036
Eastern Michigan U.	6,957	7,190	21,149	629	814
Florida Atlantic U.	2,173	1,341	6,235	259	315
Florida State U.	8,571	7,082	18,167	1,050	1,087†
Illinois State U.	5,656	6,754	15,535	620	701
Indiana U., including	23,649	18,205	53,575	2,052*	5,294*
Iowa State U.	12,652	5,442	19,172	1,080	1,586
Kansas State U.	7,601	4,433	13,149	639	1,123
Kent State U.	11,681	9,485	28,731	989	1,293
Lousiana State U., including	(15,427)	(9,928)	(32,601)	(1,960*)	(4,288*)
Louisiana State U., Baton Rouge	9,200	5,761	18,587	1,200*	2,600*
Louisiana State U., New Orleans	4,352	3,345	10,283	325*	550*
U. of Arkansas at Little Rock	1,115	743	3,432	110	140
U. of California, including			(106,274)		
U. of Calif., Berkeley			28,088		
U. of Calif., Davis			12,583		
U. of Calif., Irvine			5,055		
U. of Calif., Los Angeles			30,936		
U. of Calif., Riverside			5,360		
U. of Calif., San Diego			4,838		
U. of Calif., San Francisco			2,523		
U. of Calif., Santa Barbara			13,734		
U. of Calif., Santa Cruz			3,157		
U. of Cincinnati	13,276	6,831	35,174	1,399	2,698
U. of Colorado	12,307	7,725	28,064	1,482	2,546
U. of Connecticut	8,991	6,046	18,670	1,125*	
U. of Delaware	4,844	3,870	14,386	538	825
U. of Florida	12,512	6,699	22,603	2,404	3,100
U. of Georgia	10,867	7,021	21,590	1,300	1,750
U. of Hawaii	7,927	7,401	18,474	1,023	1,574
U. of Houston	10,091	5,112	24,383	724	1,333
U. of Idaho	3,773	1,665	6,387	413	510
U. of Illinois, including	(30,227)	(16,065)	(54,076)	(4,040*)	(7,897*)
Urbana-Champaign Campus	18,804	9,965	34,759	2,672*	4,871*
Chicago Circle Campus	9,348	5,433	16,384	975*	1,036*
Medical Center, Chicago	2,075	667	2,933	393*	1,990*
U. of Iowa	10,504	6,790	20,236	1,099	2,518
U. of Kansas	9,461	6,308	19,001	1,245	—

Institution					
Louisiana State U., Medical Center	612	142	807	300*	1,000*
Louisiana State U., Alexandria	489	289	1,031	40*	40*
Louisiana State U., Eunice	209	93	458	30*	30*
Louisiana State U., Shreveport	565	298	1,435	65*	68*
Miami U.	6,916	5,333	15,370	699	1,143
Michigan State U., including	21,879	17,365	50,085	2,341	3,672
Oakland U.	(2,432)	(2,427)	(5,811)	(247)	(278)
Mississippi State U.	5,759	1,811	9,095	616	777
Montana State U.	4,682	2,650	7,762	440	625
New Mexico State U.	4,482	1,848	7,608	332	519
North Dakota State U.	4,324	1,785	6,905	347	535
North Texas State	7,223	4,923	15,015	591	901
Northern Illinois U.	8,448	8,752	24,555	1,196	1,288
Ohio State U.	28,261	16,299	49,132	745	
Ohio U.	9,681	7,037	17,880	633	1,229
Oklahoma State U.	10,467	5,559	20,230	837	1,244
Oregon State U.	9,565	4,932	15,200		1,335
Pennsylvania State U.	25,231	10,533	49,859	3,200*	5,950
Purdue U.	19,150	8,076	36,888	2,196	4,247
Rutgers—The State U. (including Douglass C., Colleges in Newark & C. of S. Jersey)	13,009	6,451	31,096	1,892	3,647
Southern Illinois U.	17,254	10,617	36,446		
State U. of New York	100,300	78,807	286,707		
Texas Southern U.	1,911	1,674	4,754	225	243
Texas Tech U.	10,122	6,428	19,490	839	1,304
U. of Akron	6,197	3,221	16,713	431	1,006
U. of Alabama (including)	(9,953)	(5,797)	(21,142)	(1,355)	(1,831)
U. of Ala., University	7,246	4,419	13,358	589	923
U. of Ala., Birmingham	2,013	1,066	5,249	641*	728*
U. of Ala., Huntsville	694	312	2,535	125	180
U. of Alaska	1,049	583	2,265	168	278
U. of Arizona	10,771	6,840	24,822	1,245	2,160
U. of Arkansas	6,778	3,747	11,081	662	962
U. of Kentucky	8,991	5,623	16,201	890	1,164
U. of Louisville	3,997	1,438	9,043	592	1,263
U. of Maine	5,660	3,613	16,198	634	928
U. of Maryland	21,063	14,474	48,203	1,781	3,329
U. of Massachusetts, including	(11,950)	(8,445)	(22,184)	(1,230)	(2,195)
U. of Mass. at Amherst	10,022	6,850	18,587	1,005	1,964
U. of Mass. at Boston	1,928	1,595	3,597	225	231
U. of Michigan	18,936	11,289	38,328	2,488	4,383
U. of Minnesota	31,373	19,042	70,234		
U. of Mississippi	4,560	2,305	7,654	373	531
U. of Missouri, including Columbia Campus	(24,115)	(12,312)	(47,170)	(2,689)	(5,314)
Columbia Campus	11,806	7,430	21,082	1,562	3,208
Kansas City Campus	3,903	2,078	9,674	412	1,065
Rolla Campus	4,787	210	6,308	393	620
St. Louis Campus	3,619	2,594	10,106	322	421
U. of Montana	4,780	2,457	8,443	392	687
U. of Nebraska	10,829	5,761	20,334		
U. of Nevada, including Reno Campus	(4,981)	(3,050)	(10,280)	(504†)	
Reno Campus	3,185	2,014	6,163	332†	
Las Vegas Campus	1,796	1,036	4,117	172†	
U. of New Hampshire	4,355	3,136	9,900	518	834
U. of New Mexico	7,004	4,386	15,692	652	817
U. of North Carolina, Consolidated	(22,845)	(11,912)	(40,923)	(2,299)	(3,920)
N.Car. State U. at Raleigh	8,703	1,260	12,691	682	1,254
U. of N. Car. at Chapel Hill	11,074	4,430	16,430	975	1,900
U. of N. Car. at Charlotte	1,369	942	3,085	144	180
U. of N. Car. at Greensboro	551	4,458	6,423	366	420
U. of N. Car. at Asheville	353	340	869	54	68
U. of N. Car. at Wilmington	795	482	1,425	78	98
U. of North Dakota	4,831	2,843	8,168	442	760
U. of Oklahoma	11,249	6,358	20,658	625	1,185*
U. of Oregon	7,755	5,103	15,266	685*	815*
U. of South Carolina	8,518	4,737	15,607	601	1,079
U. of South Dakota	2,844	1,504	5,856	276	404
U. of South Florida	6,640	4,460	15,450	620	638

I. UNIVERSITIES AND LARGE INSTITUTIONS OF COMPLEX ORGANIZATION (*Continued*)
1. Under Public Control

Institution	Men Full-time	Women Full-time	Grand Total Students	Full-time Teaching Staff	Total Teaching Staff
U. of Tennessee, including ___	(17,342)	(10,066)	(36,320)	(2,117)	(3,748)
U. of Tenn., Knoxville ___	12,206	6,943	26,794	1,286	2,253
U. of Tenn., Martin ___	2,315	1,627	4,208	239	248
U. of Tenn., Chattanooga ___	1,567	1,156	3,658	174	191
U. of Tenn., Medical Units ___	1,254	340	1,660	418	1,056
U. of Texas (inc. all campuses)	33,750	17,911	64,572	3,302	4,803
U. of Toledo ___	6,125	2,935	14,154	532	612
U. of Utah ___	10,160	5,148	20,543	827	1,323
U. of Vermont ___	3,612	2,656	6,745	607	856
U. of Virginia at Charlottesville M	7,706	975	9,735	650	850
U. of Washington ___	16,693	10,216	32,749	1,855	3,086
U. of Wisconsin, including ___	(30,567)	(19,937)	(68,109)	—	—
U. of Wisc., Madison ___	19,195	12,396	35,549	—	—
U. of Wisc., Milwaukee ___	6,358	4,657	18,978	—	—
U. of Wisc., Green Bay ___	1,794	967	3,419	—	—
U. of Wisc., Parkside ___	1,211	684	2,911	—	—
U. of Wisc., Center System ___	2,009	1,233	4,400	—	—
U. of Wisc., Extension ___	—	2,559	2,852	—	—
Utah State U. ___	4,571	4,632	9,419	429	579
Washington State U. ___	6,727	8,541	13,191	—	—
Wayne State U. ___	12,934	5,206	34,924	1,286	2,654
West Virginia U. ___	9,576	7,583	19,119	1,091	1,341
Western Michigan U. ___	9,132	—	21,858	833	1,100
Wichita State U. ___	4,734	2,476	12,296	411	800
Wisconsin State University System ___	(31,176)	(23,617)	(61,890)	—	—
Stout State U. ___	2,829	2,070	5,247	—	—
Wisc. S. U.—Eau Claire ___	3,267	3,683	7,846	—	—
Wisc. S. U.—La Crosse ___	3,123	2,770	6,659	—	—
Wisc. S. U.—Oshkosh ___	5,329	4,447	11,656	—	—
Wisc. S. U.—Platteville ___	3,388	1,536	5,396	—	—
Wisc. S. U.—River Falls ___	2,338	1,329	4,123	—	—
Wisc. S. U.—Stevens Point ___	4,314	3,002	8,061	—	—
Wisc. S. U.—Superior ___	1,744	977	3,143	—	—
Wisc. S. U.—Whitewater ___	4,844	3,803	9,759	—	—
Totals	1,084,429	695,958	2,525,259	88,154	143,899

* Approximate
† Full-time equivalents

I. UNIVERSITIES AND LARGE INSTITUTIONS OF COMPLEX ORGANIZATION

2. Under Private Control

Institution	Men Full-time	Women Full-time	Grand Total Students	Full-time Teaching Staff	Total Teaching Staff
American U.	2,910	2,714	15,347	324	724
Baylor U.	2,894	2,649	6,121	298	397
Boston C.	6,023	2,182	10,214	762	1,185
Boston U.	7,792	9,298	23,826	1,139	2,200*
Brigham Young U.	12,021	10,118	25,615	909	1,463
Brown U. (inc. Pembroke C.)	3,734	1,437	5,542	571	1,160*
Case Western Reserve U.	5,217	2,256	9,951	1,230	4,200
Catholic U. of America	2,443	1,703	6,161	526	811
Clark U., Mass.	1,147	741	3,169	110	216
Columbia U.	9,317	2,582	16,580	2,400*	4,500*
Cornell U.	10,703	3,371	14,624	1,509	1,821
Creighton U.	2,398	1,180	4,234	334	687
Dartmouth M	3,138	72	3,230	278	460
DePaul U.	3,715	1,323	8,581	306	523
Drake U.	2,663	1,850	7,431	266	407
Duke U.	4,881	2,341	7,662	1,034	—
Duquesne U.	3,287	2,029	7,366	312	434
Emory U.	3,242	1,477	5,041	742	1,637
Fairleigh Dickinson U.	4,562	3,042	19,704	465	1,135
Fordham U.	5,423	2,283	11,229	480	641
George Washington U.	4,598	3,018	19,535	726	1,927
Georgetown U., D. C.	5,126	1,458	7,942	794	1,816
Harvard U. (inc. Radcliffe C.)	12,760	2,646	15,406	—	7,662
Howard U.	4,263	2,993	8,596	—	—
Johns Hopkins U.	3,661	524	9,983	920¹	1,911¹
Lehigh U. M	3,663	67	5,020	286	456
Long Island U. (inc. all campuses)	8,497	3,900	20,576	795	1,359
Loyola U., Ill.	5,787	2,780	14,445	565	1,650
Loyola U., La.	1,860	957	4,923	194	350*
Marquette U.	5,034	2,762	10,636	553	983
New York U.	10,904	5,617	33,421	2,650	5,860
Northeastern U.	11,146	4,224	37,134	857	2,498
Northwestern U.	8,342	3,683	15,280	1,037	2,375
Princeton U.	4,622	351	4,973	621	1,536
Rice U.	2,339	751	3,163	440	440
Roosevelt U.	1,868	1,036	6,690	186	391
St. John's U., N. Y.	6,116	3,053	13,207	490	640
St. Louis U.	5,392	2,296	11,232	808	1,711
Southern Methodist U.	4,035	2,415	9,878	450	670
Stanford U.	7,526	2,619	12,385	1,020	1,268
Syracuse U.	8,701	5,436	24,071	2,064	3,234
Temple U.	10,220	6,359	32,973		
Texas Christian U.	2,432	2,149	6,463	311	460
Tufts U. (inc. Jackson C.)	3,091	1,413	5,010	635	1,015
Tulane U. (inc. Newcomb C.)	4,608	1,768	8,137	663	810
Union C., N. Y.	1,647	0	3,184	133	136
U. of Bridgeport	2,421	2,398	8,838	343	493
U. of Chicago	4,697	3,106	9,136	1,157	—
U. of Dayton	5,120	2,552	9,770	363	555
U. of Denver	4,509	3,007	9,375	469	763
U. of Detroit	4,212	1,416	9,319	312	600
U. of Hartford	2,246	1,361	8,855	245	249
U. of Miami	8,165	3,638	16,474	942	1,160
U. of Notre Dame	7,451	212	7,924	652	823
U. of Pennsylvania	10,379	3,522	18,222	1,703	4,691
U. of Pittsburgh	10,286	6,158	28,426	1,460	2,022
U. of Richmond	2,183	647	4,208	216	307
U. of Rochester	3,824	2,004	8,438	980	1,775
U. of Southern California	8,536	3,735	20,016	1,140	2,170
U. of Tulsa	2,154	1,878	6,540	177	380
Vanderbilt U.	4,139	1,625	5,963	876	1,236
Washington U.	4,769	2,558	11,257	878	1,994
Yale U.	7,639	1,451	9,341	1,350	2,750
Yeshiva U.	2,247	896	4,609	986	1,896
Totals	340,725	161,067	752,602	45,442	89,623

* Approximate
¹ 1968-69

TABLE 2
COLLEGES OF ARTS AND SCIENCES

Institution	Men Full-time	Women Full-time	Grand Total Students	Full-time Teaching Staff	Total Teaching Staff
Abilene Christian	1,468	1,192	3,110	149	178
Adelphi	1,592	1,811	4,507	304	554
Adrian	738	690	1,478	86	104
Agnes Scott *W*	0	721	725	78	86
Alabama Ag. & M. *Pub.*	796	1,145	2,286	144	155
Alaska Methodist U.	210	171	787	35	60
Albertus Magnus *W*	0	563	584	30	60
Albion	944	855	1,822	125	145
Albright	649	542	1,524	83	98
Alderson-Broaddus	488	444	943	56	80
Alfred U.	1,226	570	1,994	162	187
Allegheny	944	646	1,659	112	114
Alma	624	612	1,264	73	74
Alvernia *W*	0	153	263	16	26
Alverno *W*	3	641	881	64	85
American International *M*	1,101	619	3,212	90	105
Amherst *M*	1,213	23	1,243	126	147
Anderson	813	668	1,701	80	111
Andrews U.	716	649	1,499	133	163
Angelo S. C. *Pub.*	1,717	1,144	3,448	110	130
Anna Maria *W*	0	616	647	46	65
Annhurst *W*	0	403	457	10	45
Antioch	1,216	892	2,131	107	154
Aquinas	469	546	1,473	89	109
Arkansas	230	107	352	23	26
Arkansas Ag., Mech. & Normal *Pub.*	1,700	1,654	3,411	166	171
Arkansas Poly. *Pub.*	1,595	815	2,540	116	116
Arkansas S. U. *Pub.*	3,677	2,311	7,199	296	310
Armstrong S. C. *Pub.*	654	551	2,168	—	—
Asbury	445	577	1,031	62	73
Ashland	1,228	1,208	2,817	155	163
Assumption *M*	777	152	1,690	59	88
Athenaeum of Ohio *M*	356	0	356	29	39
Athens	636	192	1,273	51	79
Atlanta U.	196	315	1,025	87	120
Atlantic Christian	770	620	1,544	69	91

Institution	Men Full-time	Women Full-time	Grand Total Students	Full-time Teaching Staff	Total Teaching Staff
Brescia	335	297	950	57	81
Briar Cliff, Iowa	361	536	1,067	58	74
Briarcliff, N. Y. *W*	0	648	668	50	72
Bridgewater	445	379	842	60	70
Bryn Mawr *W*	93	971	1,328	137	202
Bucknell U.	1,740	970	2,845	196	233
Buena Vista	481	265	930	52	57
Butler U.	1,146	1,195	4,184	141	204
Cabrini *W*	0	395		31	38
Caldwell C. for *W*	0	572	652	49	65
California Baptist	274	282	677	28	45
California Lutheran	493	509	1,174	64	76
California State Colleges	(79,750)	(59,350)	(265,537)*	(3,767)*	(10,052)*
Dominguez Hills	761	725	1,915	34	94
Calif. S. C. at Fullerton	4,450	3,120	13,200	250	465
Calif. S. C. at Hayward	3,717	2,627	12,650	157	435
Calif. S. C. at Long Beach	9,191	6,309	26,844	409	1,057
Calif. S. C. at Los Angeles	6,390	4,524	25,250	433	889
Calif. S. C. at San Bernardino	689	585	1,784	11	97
Calif. S. Poly. C., Kellogg-Voorhis	5,220	1,932	8,305	45	386
Calif. S. Poly. C., San Luis Obispo	7,232	2,983	11,350	92	631
Chico S. C.	4,451	3,873	9,951	134	510
Fresno S. C.	5,933	4,019	18,628	165	701
Humboldt S. C.	2,977	1,459	5,774	71	301
Sacramento S. C.	5,259	3,781	18,127	203	654
San Diego S. C.	3,728	3,450	23,676	600	978
San Fernando Valley S. C.	2,237	5,341	22,285	341	798
San Francisco S. C.	5,866	5,519	25,346	412	874
San Jose S. C.	9,259	7,325	32,351	336	874
Sonoma S. C.	1,465	1,154	5,230	46	204

Institution	1	2	3	4	5
Atlantic Union	324	321	756	52	75
Augsburg *Pub.*	878	826	1,786	87	125
Augustana, Ill.	725	908	2,672	102	129
Augustana, S. D.	893	799	2,078	102	133
Aurora	951	431	1,329	141	162
Austin	300	594	1,072	50	111
Avila *W*	441	12	547	77	88
Azusa Pacific	398	414	912	43	55
Baker U.	327	494	882	41	55
Baldwin-Wallace	1,149	1,236	3,153	69	76
Barber-Scotia	378	166	560	133	181
Bard	330	326	678	45	54
Barnard *W*	1,882	0	1,894	53	72
Barrington	310	259	617	141	193
Barry *W*	740	20	1,339	34	59
Bates	491	617	1,124	80	132
Beaver *W*	818	50	891	75	80
Belhaven	293	262	631	59	84
Bellarmine-Ursuline	338	995	1,876	40	51
Belmont	438	459	986	86	125
Belmont Abbey *M*	7	746	775	52	65
Beloit	904	845	1,773	43	54
Benedict *W*	742	510	1,259	128	140
Bennett *W*	626	0	627	79	87
Bennington *W*	505	47	554	62	71
Berea	713	670	1,399	59	66
Berry	521	547	1,174	97	136
Bethany, Kansas	282	366	664	66	74
Bethany, W. Va.	435	568	1,016	39	48
Bethany Nazarene	553	595	1,548	69	84
Bethel, Kansas	231	288	549	75	87
Bethel, Minn.	540	447	1,034	38	71
Bethel, Tenn.	141	436	678	56	87
Bethune-Cookman	610	507	1,138	38	47
Biola	643	625	1,436	55	59
Birmingham-Southern	485	487	1,005	78	103
Biscayne *M*	0	416	416	82	88
Bishop	850	956	1,960	29	30
Blackburn	286	311	612	133	136
Bloomfield	302	737	1,541	37	40
Blue Mountain *W*	270	28	325	66	87
Bluffton	353	386	771	28	34
Boise S. C. *Pub.*	1,575	3,110	7,080	47	64
Borromeo Seminary of Ohio *M*	0	204	207	247	322
Bowdoin *M*	13	948	966	12	26
Bradley U.	1,695	3,240	6,099	110	133
Brandeis U.	1,097	1,100	2,268	361	441
Brenau *W*	506		575	315	396

Institution	1	2	3	4	5
Stanislaus S. C.	925	624	2,871	28	104
Calvin	1,830	1,602	3,572	165	202
Campbell	1,446	794	2,306	120	129
Campbellsville	463	357	882	52	58
Canisius	2,129	589	3,861	161	238
Capital U.	948	800	1,899	124	137
Cardinal Cushing *W*		393	398	33	54
Cardinal Stritch *W*	0	283	660	38	54
Carleton	857	590	1,450	115	140
Carlow *W*		799	1,101	72	110
Carroll, Mont.	603	414	1,072	63	65
Carroll, Wisc.	623	600	1,247	82	98
Carson-Newman	868	829	1,814	98	120
Carthage	674	564	1,931	84	113
Catawba	556	474	1,046	72	76
Catherine Spalding *W*	35	768	1,622	117	155
Catholic U. of Puerto Rico	2,009	2,594	6,505	287	449
Cedar Crest *W*	0	720	786	58	64
Centenary C. of La.	485	370	1,056	77	110
Central, Iowa	682	577	1,283	80	92
Central Methodist, Mo.	498	352	872	62	66
Centre C. of Ky.	420	324	749	61	65
Chaminade C. of Honolulu	413	307	891	42	69
Chapman	759	903	3,522	104	250
Chatham *W*	0	605	620	54	73
Chestnut Hill *W*	0	620	1,175	51	65
Christian Brothers *M*	1,021	0	1,113	70	78
Church C. of Hawaii	563	560	1,192	68	97
Citadel *M Pub.*	2,061	122	2,586	148	151
Claflin	253	447	708	42	52
Claremont Men's C.	819	0	820	85	97
Claremont University Center	306	83	739	44	250
Clark, Ga.	376	666	1,072	105	111
Clarke *W*	10	800	942	70	95
Cleveland State U.	4,399	2,224	13,073	338	593
Coe	483	427	983	75	97
Coker *W*	3	315	339	32	37
Colby	799	707	1,531	110	125
Colgate U. *M*	2,023	38	2,090	173	188
C. Misericordia *W*	0	878	1,016	83	101
C. of Charleston *Pub.*	270	227	561	30	36
C. of Emporia	874	205	1,116	49	53
C. of Great Falls	394	303	1,159	40	64

Colleges of Arts and Sciences *(Continued)*

Institution	Men Full-time	Women Full-time	Grand Total Students	Full-time Teach-ing Staff	Total Teach-ing Staff
C. of the Holy Names *W*	3	586	983	54	104
C. of Idaho	533	351	1,092	56	70
C. of Mt. St. Joseph on the Ohio *W*	4	837	907	77	91
C. of Mt. St. Vincent *W*	0	952	984	66	80
C. of New Rochelle *W*	0	845	942	80	103
C. of Notre Dame, Calif. *W*	47	370	1,361	45	116
C. of Notre Dame of Maryland *W*	1	680	894	58	73
C. of Our Lady of the Elms *W*	0	621	621	48	75
C. of the Ozarks	321	209	539	31	34
C. of the Sacred Heart *W*	0	482	556	25	48
C. of St. Benedict *W*	0	584	627	55	60
C. of St. Catherine *W*	1	1,225	1,338	108	128
C. of St. Elizabeth *W*	0	700	817	61	109
C. of St. Francis *W*	0	714	846	49	66
C. of St. Mary *W*	0	358	449	34	46
C. of St. Rose *W*	52	748	1,348	69	102
C. of St. Scholastica *W*	42	527	639	58	80
C. of St. Teresa *W*	1	1,087	1,188	109	134
C. of St. Thomas *M*	2,024	18	2,413	108	143
C. of Santa Fe	857	205	1,357	58	79
C. of Steubenville	681	401	1,333	64	85
C. of William and Mary *Pub.*	2,167	1,668	7,253	289	343
C. of Wooster	891	735	1,683	138	142
Colorado	1,043	699	1,761	122	162
Columbia *W*	4	817	870	51	69
Columbia Union	371	353	923	61	88
Concordia, Moorhead, Minn.	1,142	1,237	2,405	148	181
Concordia, St. Paul, Minn.	358	425	800	54	69
Concordia Senior C., Ind. *M*	410	0	414	40	40
Erskine	408	322	747	48	61
Eureka	318	214	535	42	42
Evangel	435	484	977	40	61
Fairfield U. *M*	1,838	0	1,840	129	142
Findlay	758	420	1,294	54	77
Fisk U.	459	768	1,238	89	109
Florida Presbyterian	458	494	969	69	74
Florida Southern	684	698	1,516	106	116
Fontbonne *W*	2	733	826	68	92
Fort Hayes Kansas S. C. *Pub.*	2,754	1,881	5,578	232	299
Fort Lewis *Pub.*	1,089	659	1,871	86	89
Fort Wright *W*	18	261	447	38	55
Francis T. Nicholls S. C. *Pub.*	2,296	1,506	4,837	158	214
Franklin, Ind	524	250	786	56	64
Franklin and Marshall *M*	1,703	129	2,576	148	159
Franklin-Pierce	854	187	1,126	69	79
Friends U.	497	376	1,030	60	61
Furman U.	1,002	840	2,098	122	138
Gannon *M*	2,137	217	3,732	121	154
Geneva	798	586	1,654	82	127
Georgetown, Ky. *M*	642	712	1,476	87	99
Georgia C. at Milledgeville *Pub.*	487	1,100	1,710	100	106
Georgia Southwestern *Pub.*	1,304	806	2,250		
Georgian Court *W*	0	645	704	44	52
Gettysburg	1,281	602	1,895	136	160
Goddard	408	507	1,103	85	88
Gonzaga U.	1,408	849	2,701	143	208
Good Counsel *W*	0	420	461	33	52
Gordon	528	391	1,057	54	68
Goshen	517	659	1,293	69	100
Goucher *W*	2	1,039	1,064	82	111
Graceland	582	596	1,267	67	85
Grand Canyon	266	224	756	32	39
Grand Valley S. C. *Pub.*	1,373	1,095	2,718	116	132
Greensboro *Pub.*	161	491	676	51	63
Greenville	372	355	772	46	55
Grinnell	620	538	1,174	109	126

College					
Grove City	1,372	669	2,052	100	114
Guilford	709	480	1,782	91	127
Gustavus Adolphus	854	1,012	1,883	124	140
Gwynedd-Mercy W	0	561	1,020	69	115
Hamilton M	892	0	892	81	82
Hamline U.	618	618	1,272	79	104
Hampden-Sydney M	644	0	644	45	55
Hampton Institute	940	1,236	2,369	190	200
Hanover	528	476	1,020	71	74
Hardin-Simmons U.	638	620	1,768	92	104
Harding	941	882	1,888	98	101
Hartwick	812	867	1,692	106	113
Hastings	452	370	853	57	61
Haverford M	639	17	665	55	94
Heidelberg	604	582	1,223	93	117
Hendrix	522	391	914	47	50
High Point	534	560	1,124	60	73
Hillsdale	587	505	1,164	57	63
Hiram	610	511	1,145	82	96
Hobart and William Smith	1,063	448	1,520	94	123
Hofstra U.	3,897	2,677	12,373	400	679
Hollins W	15	990	1,038	82	95
Holy Family, Pa. W	0	386	700	36	57
Holy Family, Wisc.					
Hood W	17	245	585	33	46
Hope	0	645	654	62	71
Houghton	973	977	2,033	112	142
Houston Baptist	498	636	1,170	78	86
Howard Payne	351	501	1,089	50	63
Huntingdon	717	543	1,429	74	79
Huntington, Ind.	286	440	823	52	61
Huron	271	224	535	31	49
Huston-Tillotson	414	187	702	38	42
Idaho S. U. Pub.	267	352	641	45	57
Illinois	3,108	1,670	6,162	318	423
Illinois Wesleyan U.	507	317	920	43	54
Immaculata W	791	847	1,684	120	134
Immaculate Heart W	0	916	1,448	87	102
Incarnate Word W	22	391	931	59	78
Indiana Central	28	779	1,303	82	112
Iona M	553	485	2,333	68	112
Iowa Wesleyan	2,105	217	3,415	150	188
Ithaca	500	329	981	61	64
Jacksonville U.	1,673	2,022	3,761	218	307
Jamestown	1,289	844	2,963	124	161
	357	248	635	41	65

College					
Connecticut W	51	1,416	1,695	142	175
Converse W	3	804	871	68	88
Cornell, Iowa	520	466	995	86	92
Culver-Stockton	510	286	844	38	53
Cumberland	1,095	681	1,873	79	95
Dakota Wesleyan U.	372	240	740	39	53
Dana	489	399	1,057	45	52
David Lipscomb	1,081	1,052	2,205	102	111
Davidson M	1,016	0	1,018	89	89
Davis and Elkins	454	313	791	48	59
Defiance	670	367	1,096	70	84
Delaware S. C. Pub.	636	460	1,261	81	101
Denison U.	1,157	940	2,131	155	180
DePauw U.	1,230	1,173	2,439	160	193
Detroit Inst. of Tech.	585	93	1,285	51	95
Dickinson	956	615	1,633	125	134
Dillard U.	299	610	922	78	80
Doane	484	253	754	45	51
Dominican, Texas W	9	281	440	49	69
Dominican, Wisc.	231	303	693	45	63
Dominican, C. of San Rafael W	10	368	749	48	83
Don Bosco M	119	0	126	5	12
Drew U.	688	647	1,478	103	153
Dropsie U.	146	14	160	14	22
Drury	546	483	2,344	81	173
Dunbarton C. of the Holy Cross W	0	410	460	37	60
D'Youville W	0	1,250	1,287	96	121
Earlham	576	478	1,098	89	119
East Texas Baptist	335	328	755	33	44
Eastern Baptist	252	283	562	40	59
Eastern Kentucky U. Pub.	4,778	3,705	9,664	495	671
Eastern Mennonite	429	490	939	65	88
Eastern Nazarene	374	370	783	52	67
Eastern New Mexico U. Pub.	3,017	2,440	7,644	185	311
Edgecliff W	1	625	884	55	85
Edgewood C. of the Sacred Heart W	44	413	576	46	66
Elizabethtown	788	679	1,866	104	130
Elmhurst	966	760	2,912	113	176
Elmira W	111	1,231	2,674	73	138
Elon	1,093	564	1,843	84	95
Emmanuel W	0	1,471	1,600	82	137
Emory and Henry	453	350	827	60	70

Colleges of Arts and Sciences (*Continued*)

Institution	Men Full-time	Women Full-time	Grand Total Students	Full-time Teaching Staff	Total Teaching Staff
Jarvis Christian	241	305	554	36	48
John Brown U.	408	337	768	56	63
John Carroll U.	2,377	416	4,369	189	299
Johnson C. Smith U.	536	628	1,244	73	88
Judson W	3	408	454	27	41
Juniata	672	482	1,204	85	94
Kalamazoo W	708	606	1,337	75	101
Kansas S. C., Pitts-burg Pub.	3,022	1,724	6,207	299	327
Kansas Wesleyan U.	463	221	717	38	45
Kentucky Wesleyan	472	261	974	57	65
Kenyon W	813	156	970	93	94
Keuka W	1	826	840	59	63
King	186	117	317	35	41
King's, Pa. M	1,619	6	2,038	107	123
King's, The, N.Y.	319	439	773	65	81
Knox	851	612	1,488	90	105
Knoxville	377	520	918	65	92
Ladycliff W	0	458	532	42	53
Lafayette M	1,824	0	2,070	164	173
LaGrange M	275	276	584	38	43
LaSalle M	3,457	0	6,634	140	300
LaVerne W	324	290	668	44	66
Lake Erie W	19	553	794	46	80
Lake Forest	663	620	1,350	105	116
Lake Superior S. C. Pub.	949	325	1,651	84	100
Lakeland	425	220	666	37	42
Lambuth	399	360	773	55	66
Lander	273	391	688	36	40
Lane	409	567	976	48	51
Langston U.	570	558	1,225	70	76
Lawrence Inst. of Tech.	1,936	45	4,561	65	183
Lawrence U.	699	607	1,331	128	134
Le Moyne, N. Y.	1,021	598	1,639	92	125
LeMoyne-Owen, Tenn.	215	416	703	34	48
Lebanon Valley	533	392	1,440	65	76
Lenoir Rhyne	622	673	1,314	90	103
Lewis M	1,610	64	2,321	78	101
Lewis and Clark	858	853	2,001	112	139

Institution	Men Full-time	Women Full-time	Grand Total Students	Full-time Teaching Staff	Total Teaching Staff
Sacred Heart W.	7	364	440	32	53
Maryville, Tenn.	357	349	714	56	67
Marywood W	28	1,330	1,818	106	144
McMurry	663	544	1,646	73	82
McNeese S. C. Pub.	2,424	1,671	5,070	208	274
McPherson	450	250	745	44	51
Memphis S. U. Pub.	6,784	5,023	17,763	639	1,126
Mercer U.	1,154	618	1,945	121	133
Mercy C. of Detroit	113	774	1,118	73	96
Mercy, N. Y. W	86	564	954	57	74
Mercyhurst W	26	602	689	48	62
Meredith W	0	930	946	59	73
Messiah	262	287	582	50	65
Methodist	473	394	894	48	55
Middle Tenn. S. U. Pub.	3,499	2,762	7,425	345	425
Middlebury	917	690	1,624	135	157
Midland Lutheran	411	315	906	51	57
Midwestern U.	1,559	1,033	4,008	128	176
Milligan	449	380	863	53	54
Millikin U.	791	611	1,883	91	127
Mills W	15	792	833	63	99
Millsaps	474	431	979	62	79
Milton	480	179	689	38	47
Mississippi S. C. for W Pub.	889	569	2,359	89	110
Missouri Southern Pub.	0	2,325	2,633	149	167
Missouri Valley	1,491	875	3,120	116	120
Mobile	614	246	899	41	46
Molloy Catholic C. for W	213	145	406	26	28
Monmouth, Ill.	0	777	1,142	68	92
Monmouth, N. J.	769	520	1,313	85	99
Monterey Inst. of Foreign Studies	2,477	1,780	5,327	209	307
Moravian	68	50	259	17	39
Morehead	694	463	1,196	76	98
Morehouse M	955	0	982	79	90
Morgan S. C. Pub.	1,756	1,874	4,653	208	289
Morningside	669	603	1,703	68	89
Morris Brown	495	806	1,420	91	109

Institution					
Limestone	172	481	738	44	47
Lincoln Memorial U.	462	261	741	37	44
Lincoln U., Mo. *Pub.*	1,159	825	2,238	100	146
Lincoln U., Pa.	754	358	1,130	94	117
Lindenwood *W*	105	462	660	53	64
Linfield	523	439	1,067	60	86
Livingstone	344	463	808	51	69
Loma Linda U.	1,479	1,041	3,095	354	1,209
Loras *M*	1,427	0	1,666	126	132
Loretto Heights *W*	14	838	934	63	78
Louisiana	400	361	977	48	63
Loyola, Md.	995	32	2,995	70	190
Loyola U. of Los Angeles *M*	2,265	104	3,101	137	191
Luther	1,036	1,008	2,085	118	131
Lycoming	876	575	1,530	88	101
Lynchburg	787	755	1,928	117	138
Macalester	1,008	942	1,980	152	206
MacMurray	451	448	979	65	74
Madonna *W*	347	324	610	28	44
Malone	723	352	953	47	63
Manchester	3,730	728	1,489	76	81
Manhattan *M*	4	29	4,706	237	308
Manhattanville *W*	399	1,162	1,479	77	115
Marian, Ind.	0	523	1,105	60	90
Marian C. of Fond du Lac, Wisc. *W*	348	303	431	34	46
Marion, Ind.	1,072	337	848	33	49
Marietta	1,211	711	2,226	104	115
Marillac *W*	124	255	368	29	44
Marist	696	120	1,713	60	90
Marlboro	3,189	91	217	16	32
Mars Hill	0	521	1,257	96	102
Marshall U. *Pub.*	119	3,189	9,463	57	440•
Mary Baldwin *W*	7	699	707	57	62
Mary Hardin-Baylor *W*	0	413	686	41	52
Mary Manse *W*	41	467	758	57	73
Mary Washington *W Pub.*	2	2,107	2,171	152	180
Maryerest *W*	0	683	1,100	59	69
Marygrove *W*		737	950	71	86
Marylhurst *W*		358	675	44	64
Marymount C. at Loyola U., Calif. *W*	7	656	829	32	41
Marymount, Kansas	82	405	590	56	66
Marymount, N.Y.	0				
Marymount Manhattan *W*	0	1,068	1,111	82	103
Maryville C. of the	0	611	627	38	66

Institution					
Morris Harvey	1,038	819	3,135	85	145
Mount Angel	153	145	322	35	39
Mount Holyoke *W*	8	1,817	1,833	145	185
Mount Marty *W*	27	394	475	47	56
Mount Mary *W*	0	803	919	96	112
Mount Mercy, Iowa *W*	11	351	613	28	43
Mount St. Agnes *W*	0	352	366	30	40
Mount St. Mary, N. H. *W*	39	275	298	31	41
Mount St. Mary, N. Y. *W*	81	541	687	38	55
Mount St. Mary's, Calif. *W*	1,051	761	1,459	74	129
Mount St. Mary's, Md. *M*	0	2	1,064	64	74
Mount St. Scholastica *W*	661	540	580	42	60
Mount Union	847	564	1,255	81	93
Muhlenberg	0	554	2,003	112	123
Mundelein *W*	691	815	1,245	69	96
Muskingum	546	710	1,467	100	116
Nasson	18	242	801	53	56
Nazareth, Mich. *W*	0	430	477	47	62
Nazareth C. of Rochester, N. Y. *W*	648	1,183	1,365	71	91
Nebraska Wesleyan U.	244	527	1,326	101	112
New	660	152	397	50	55
New School for Social Research	536	321	3,506	57	113
Newberry	0	271	812	60	67
Newton C. of the Sacred Heart *W*	1,667	782	809	66	99
Niagara U.	1,249	721	3,013	162	205
North Carolina Central U. *Pub.*	422	1,862	3,290	220	246
North Central	632	392	954	61	71
North Georgia	746	501	1,133	57	57
North Park	3,750	690	1,641	75	111
Northeast Louisiana S. C. *Pub.*	446	2,460	7,616	302	408
Northland	498	211	679	48	59
Northwest Nazarene	2,400	534	1,101	55	71
Northwestern S. C. of La. *Pub.*	1,275	2,002	6,017	312	463
Northwestern S. C., Okla. *Pub.*	1,179	896	2,507	98	162
Norwich U. *M*		0	1,216	125	130

Colleges of Arts and Sciences (*Continued*)

Institution	Men Full-time	Women Full-time	Grand Total Students	Full-time Teaching Staff	Total Teaching Staff
Notre Dame, Ohio W	0	481	586	36	74
Notre Dame of Staten Island W	0	417	435	35	50
Nyack Missionary	259	279	563	36	65
Oakwood	274	324	632	36	50
Oberlin	1,439	1,200	2,727	148	154
Occidental	1,052	705	1,828	121	156
Oglethorpe	674	287	1,221	38	46
Ohio Dominican	243	501	985	53	89
Ohio Northern U.	1,493	687	2,314	144	168
Ohio Wesleyan U.	1,241	1,200	2,472	174	187
Oklahoma Baptist U.	684	742	1,656	75	103
Oklahoma Christian	535	514	1,145	30	43
Oklahoma City U.	836	566	2,362	107	182
Oklahoma C. of Liberal Arts	322	492	980	50	63
Old Dominion	3,051	2,152	9,565	398	450*
Olivet	486	298	823	53	60
Olivet Nazarene	729	828	1,825	83	102
Ottawa U.	569	422	1,024	51	77
Otterbein	674	667	1,367	94	100
Ouachita Baptist U.	751	602	1,474	93	101
Our Lady of the Lake W	169	725	1,657	86	126
Pace	3,045	910	9,578	290	662
Pacific, Calif.	174	122	330	23	36
Pacific Lutheran U.	1,025	1,194	2,857	142	177
Pacific Union	871	820	1,857	111	144
Pacific U., Oregon	781	381	1,209	77	113
Paine	224	414	656	48	55
Pan American	2,061	1,469	4,612	159	179
Park	457	192	708	48	49
Pasadena	569	461	1,232	50	60
Pembroke S. U. *Pub.*	1,063	593	1,696	100	105
Pepperdine	738	385	1,999	70	131
Pfeiffer	443	356	834	64	81
Philander Smith	227	318	596	32	48
Phillips U.	540	467	1,346	85	97
Piedmont	260	225	526	36	36
Pikeville	454	352	932	52	59
Pitzer W	4	656	669	12	51

Institution	Men Full-time	Women Full-time	Grand Total Students	Full-time Teaching Staff	Total Teaching Staff
St. John's, N. Mex. W	142	115	261	32	34
St. John's U., Minn. M	1,455	0	1,544	109	131
St. Joseph's, Conn. W	0	505	905	56	87
St. Joseph, Md. W	0	525	548	52	67
St. Joseph's, East Chicago, Ind.	586	279	1,485	33	70
St. Joseph's, Rensselaer, Ind.	1,176	239	1,454	71	92
St. Joseph's, Maine W	0	168	252	26	34
St. Joseph's C. for W, N.Y.	0	562	567	65	76
St. Joseph's, Pa. M	2,406	216	6,842	152	303
St. Lawrence U.	1,152	894	2,192	146	150
St. Martin's	433	157	755	65	85
St. Mary's, Kansas W	1	493	591	41	50
St. Mary of the Plains	372	228	657	50	53
St. Mary-of-the-Woods W	0	463	475	41	64
St. Mary's, Calif. M	919	0	939	77	97
St. Mary's, Ind. W	0	1,427	1,564	112	135
St. Mary's, Minn. M	945	31	1,042	60	71
St. Mary's Dominican W	0	409	608	37	58
St. Mary's Seminary, Mo. M	76	0	79	10	12
St. Mary's U. of San Antonio	2,045	587	4,278	142	220
St. Meinrad M	253	0	259	20	38
St. Michael's M	1,231	8	1,403	94	102
St. Norbert	818	698	1,651	95	118
St. Olaf	1,320	1,264	2,593	167	216
St. Paul's, Va.	223	303	536	44	48
St. Peter's	1,885	721	4,716	154	289
St. Procopius M	723	171	969	62	74
St. Thomas Seminary M	226	0	226	10	32
St. Vincent M	906	0	942	74	86
St. Xavier W	32	625	842	71	95
Salem, N. Car. W	1	520	557	56	72

Institution					
PMC Colleges M	1,415	78	2,965	106	180
Point Park	1,775	598	3,264	168	215
Pomona	745	559	1,315	124	149
Portland S. U. Pub.	5,141	3,660	10,870	432	619
Prairie View A & M C of Texas Pub.	1,712	1,658	4,362	221	221
Pratt Inst.	1,844	1,118	4,270	175	518
Principia	354	390	754	55	69
Providence M	2,285	0	3,398	196	210
Queens W	1,069	693	708	66	70
Quincy	1,376	741	2,134	92	110
Quinnipiac	0	616	2,753	120	205
Radcliffe W	841	1,235	1,235	(	)[1]
Randolph-Macon M	0	4	847	65	72
Randolph-Macon W	737	806	820	79	89
Reed	749	527	1,379	112	132
Regis, Colorado	0	245	1,232	51	102
Regis, Mass. W	501	916	953	66	84
Ricker	646	135	643	43	43
Ripon	0	399	1,082	82	114
Rivier W	601	492	915	37	67
Roanoke	279	485	1,517	72	94
Roberts Wesleyan	366	374	717	35	70
Rockford	872	373	1,557	65	74
Rockhurst M	307	106	2,327	71	135
Rocky Mountain	764	187	529	42	54
Rollins	27	559	3,419	87	170
Rosary W	38	930	1,386	87	117
Rosary Hill W	0	1,233	1,375	79	122
Rosemont W	38	686	712	47	83
Russell W	283	53	69	5	13
Russell Sage W	194	1,430	3,253	91	164
Sacred Heart, Kansas	67	306	705	41	60
Sacred Heart Seminary M	1,095	0	194	17	24
St. Alphonsus M	1,136	0	67	15	18
St. Ambrose M	624	140	1,374	76	97
St. Anselm's	1,610	221	1,587	110	131
St. Benedict's M	605	0	1,253	59	65
St. Bernard M	313	52	715	46	57
St. Bonaventure U.	609	521	2,557	157	180
St. Edward's U.	1,697	222	851	75	85
St. Francis, Ind.	930	351	2,321	60	109
St. Francis, Maine	1,244	127	753	42	51
St. Francis, N. Y. M	285	44	2,345	91	115
St. Francis, Pa.	201	602	1,574	87	101
St. John Fisher M		0	1,244	70	85
St. John's, Calif. M		0	285	23	25
St. John's, Md.		143	347	39	51

Institution					
Salem, W. Va.	1,056	353	1,580	90	102
Salve Regina W	9	707	998	59	73
Samford U.	1,312	783	2,676	134	180
San Francisco C. for W					
Sarah Lawrence W	9	554	844	42	59
School of the Ozarks	73	604	717	74	146
Scripps W	433	373	872	36	50
Seattle U.	0	519	526	52	70
Seattle Pacific	1,409	1,162	3,468	221	242
Seminary of St. Pius X M	735	870	1,962	99	123
Seton Hall U.	55	0	55	7	12
Seton Hill W	3,847	1,407	9,696	350	599
Shaw U.	0	718	879	63	71
Shepherd Pub.	618	509	1,151	81	85
Shimer	829	680	1,707	83	85
Shorter	191	106	312	25	29
Siena, N. Y. M	235	339	638	44	51
Siena, Tenn. W	1,448	26	1,715	97	122
Siena Heights W	1	175	305	25	31
Simmons W	33	378	638	50	61
Simpson	32	1,673	2,200	153	312
Sioux Falls	507	393	926	69	78
Skidmore W	420	282	1,000	46	61
Smith W	26	1,737	1,782	148	170
Southeastern Louisiana Pub.	45	2,577	2,639	232	286
Southern California	2,981	1,875	5,552	264	
Southern Missionary	244	215	515	23	32
Southern State, Ark. Pub.	542	642	1,309	88	96
Southwest Baptist	1,136	811	2,243	102	123
Southwest Missouri S. C. Pub.	585	548	1,229	64	68
Southwestern, Kansas	3,790	2,957	8,192	375	446
Southwestern at Memphis	352	281	666	42	50
Southwestern S. C., Okla. Pub.	562	478	1,055	88	107
Southwestern U., Texas	2,734	1,785	5,070	187	205
Spelman W	438	397	863	71	75
Spring Arbor	0	974	976	83	97
Spring Hill	312	316	708	44	56
Springfield	462	358	970	76	90
Stephens W	1,454	722	2,590	111	149
Sterling	12	2,053	2,145	154	173
Stetson U.	286	232	549	35	41
	1,259	789	2,988	130	140

Colleges of Arts and Sciences *(Continued)*

Institution	Men Full-time	Women Full-time	Grand Total Students	Full-time Teach-ing Staff	Total Teach-ing Staff
Stillman	258	419	681	42	54
Stonehill	762	584	1,423	73	84
Sulpician Seminary of the Northwest M	76		76	10	20
Susquehanna U.	669	525	1,221	97	113
Swarthmore	618	491	1,114	118	152
Sweet Briar W	0	740	743	73	77
Tabor	227	187	432	26	45
Talladega	197	350	550	53	58
Tarkio	416	209	635	35	40
Tarleton S. C. Pub.	1,714	831	2,665	122	133
Taylor U.	697	688	1,409	75	87
Temple Buell W	0	1,037	1,064	84	94
Tennessee Wesleyan	368	298	752	43	52
Texas A & I U. Pub.	3,792	2,180	7,253	247	310
Texas Lutheran	412	379	843	45	55
Texas Woman's U. Pub.	0	4,098	5,318	280	291
Thiel	666	640	1,341	77	107
Thomas More	903	474	2,224	74	148
Tift W	0	635	654	27	33
Tougaloo	300	390	693	52	59
Transylvania	461	410	878	66	72
Trinity, Conn. M	1,236	159	1,876	150	161
Trinity, D. C. W	2	746	822	68	89
Trinity, U., Texas	1,090	981	2,641	168	219
Trinity, Vermont W	0	429	454	39	55
Tusculum	379	202	595	38	45
Union, Ky.	502	250	956	54	62
Union, Nebr.	423	375	892	79	82
Union U., Tenn.	374	321	778	48	51
U. of Albuquerque	499	322	1,380	57	90
U. of Corpus Christi	336	148	624	23	23
U. of Dallas	450	359	1,202	72	104
U. of Dubuque	569	283	1,048	55	61
U. of Evansville	1,503	1,430	5,369	161	262
U. of Portland	848	687	1,878	118	151
U. of Puget Sound	1,231	1,189	3,421	124	180
U. of Redlands	888	770	1,880	100	131

Institution	Men Full-time	Women Full-time	Grand Total Students	Full-time Teach-ing Staff	Total Teach-ing Staff
Va. S. C. Pub.	894	1,336	3,165	196	225
Viterbo W	3	408	447	48	66
Voorhees	285	428	714	48	55
Wabash M	861	0	866	78	
Wagner	1,191	1,167	3,124	137	201
Wake Forest U.	2,251	816	3,210	348	498
Walla Walla	760	690	1,713	87	103
Warner Pacific	175	128	378	31	48
Wartburg	678	682	1,409	78	92
Washburn U. of Topeka Pub.	2,150	1,340	4,635	118	215
Washington	318	301	637	52	61
Washington and Jefferson M	833	0	853	80	80
Washington and Lee U. M	1,417	0	1,433	137	147
Wayland Baptist	263	282	692	38	46
Waynesburg	678	396	1,090	62	77
Weber S. C. Pub.	4,528	2,239	10,522	341	355
Webster	191	515	1,317	55	97
Wellesley W	0	1,744	1,756	162	198
Wells W	0	645	647	69	86
Wesleyan C. Ga. W	0	498	514	54	60
Wesleyan U., Conn. M	1,385	0	1,714	208	258
West Texas S. U. Pub.	3,811	2,220	7,935	248	329
West Va. S. C. Pub.	1,556	838	3,710	154	173
West Va. Wesleyan	866	877	1,796	104	127
Western C. for W	0	439	439	56	67
Western Maryland	529	526	1,755	90	106
Western New England	1,101	131	3,361	69	184
Westmar	650	415	1,123	58	73
Westminster, Mo. M	646	0	671	55	63
Westminster, Pa.	833	686	1,916	109	112
Westminster, Utah	455	291	827	37	51
Westmont	391	437	847	48	58
Wheaton, Ill.	949	904	1,927	142	158
Wheaton, Mass. W	5	1,122	1,139	93	104

Institution					
U. of St. Thomas	571	347	1,101	54	88
U. of San Diego	715	425	1,398	109	123
U. of Santa Clara M	2,682	1,201	5,683	215	296
U. of Scranton M	1,618	14	2,876	120	171
U. of South Alabama Pub.	2,025	1,374	4,526	222	280
U. of Southern Mississippi Pub.	3,821	2,813	8,817	380	650
U. of Southwestern La. Pub.	4,972	3,441	9,965	504	617
U. of the Pacific	1,691	1,467	4,660	40	225
U. of the South M	795	109	906	63	74
U. of Tampa	1,413	632	2,448	88	118
Upper Iowa U.	647	330	1,032	71	74
Upsala	734	632	1,843	87	126
Ursinus	611	506	2,077	65	76
Ursuline, Ohio W	23	408	519	31	65
Valdosta S. C., Ga. Pub.	1,329	1,224	2,886	153	164
Valparaiso U.	2,082	1,952	4,549	244	302
Vassar W	47	1,573	1,673	189	216
Villa Maria W	0	550	635	53	64
Villanova U. M	5,285	867	8,769	418	570
Va. Mil. Inst. M. Pub.	1,142	0	1,167	129	129

Institution					
Wheeling	471	310	804	52	67
Whitman	626	481	1,121	79	90
Whittier	979	1,139	2,611	72	131
Whitworth	469	531	1,622	68	78
Wilberforce U.	462	496	958	48	58
Wiley	237	231	468	43	46
Wilkes	1,260	1,224	3,471	166	186
Willamette U.	1,029	567	1,633	96	127
William Carey	419	348	799	45	53
William Jewell	522	338	906	66	81
William Penn	533	262	902	53	59
William Woods W	0	844	976	46	52
Williams M	1,322	62	1,414	136	168
Wilmington, Ohio	556	348	945	52	66
Wilson W	8	606	620	62	67
Windham	580	283	880	60	69
Winthrop W Pub.	75	3,083	3,707	175	228
Wittenberg U.	1,280	1,261	3,151	179	277
Wofford M	950	0	961	65	74
Wright S. U. Pub.	2,964	1,577	9,921	289	391
Xavier U., Ohio	2,394	152	6,054	171	299
Yankton	415	128	634	42	50
Youngstown State U.	7,271	3,286	14,762		
Totals	609,702	513,902	1,509,829	68,210	95,410

* Approximate
1 Totals included with Harvard U.

TABLE 3
OTHER INDEPENDENT INSTITUTIONS
Technological and Related Schools

Institution	Men Full-time	Women Full-time	Grand Total Students	Full-time Teaching Staff	Total Teaching Staff
Air Force Inst. of Tech. M Pub. —	563	0	565	110	120
Albany C. of Pharmacy	309	135	444	19	29
Albany Law School	331	29	360	12	16
Albany Medical C. M	297	32	338	275	908
Alcorn A. & M. Pub.	1,042	1,334	2,421	125	137
Arkansas A. & M. Pub.	1,119	623	1,924	94	99
Armstrong	312	104	466	30	34
Babson Inst. M	951	13	1,494	42	50
Brooks Inst.	494	36	542	26	33
Bryant	1,684	304	3,498	70	120
Calif. C. of Podiatric Medicine	199	3	202	16	42
Calif. Inst. of Tech. M	1,463	39	1,537	247	575
Carnegie-Mellon U. Pub.	2,927	1,087	5,254	508	588
Clarkson C. of Tech.	2,615	58	2,757	187	220
Clemson U. Pub.	5,360	1,005	7,021	453	789
Colorado School of Mines Pub.	1,485	29	1,670	125	129
Cooper Union	726	183	1,161	79	187
Delaware Valley C. of Sc. & Ag. M	890	5	1,185	61	78
Drexel Inst. of Tech.	4,576	1,178	9,148	314	618
Embry-Riddle Aeronautical Inst.	950	13	978	36	46
Florida A. & M. U. Pub.	1,922	1,710	4,680	250	294
Florida Inst. of Tech.	1,036	55	1,979	34	154
General Motors Inst.	2,917	14	2,931	230	230
Georgia Inst. of Tech. M Pub.	7,130	164	8,249	550	800
Georgia S. C. Pub.	4,021	2,657	12,197	480	613
Golden Gate	908	95	3,083	22	204
Harvey Mudd	354	23	380	52	69

Institution	Men Full-time	Women Full-time	Grand Total Students	Full-time Teaching Staff	Total Teaching Staff
N. Carolina Ag. & Tech. S. U. Pub.	2,005	1,342	3,714	251	288
Northrop Inst. of Tech. M	1,165	9	1,323	55	71
Okla. Panhandle S. C. of Ag. & Ap. Sc. Pub.	783	424	1,338	61	73
Pennsylvania C. of Optometry	408	13	421	22	56
Philadelphia C. of Pharmacy & Sc.	654	217	977	50	108
Poly. Inst. of Brooklyn M	2,057	53	4,705	310	496
Rensselaer Poly. Inst. M	4,184	200	6,037	354	626
Rider	2,100	1,467	6,000	178	273
Rochester Inst. of Tech.	3,410	735	11,405	334	793
Rose Poly. Inst. M	868	0	1,050	—	70
St. Louis C. of Pharmacy	377	91	478	22	26
S. Carolina S. C. Pub.	838	895	2,191	121	131
S. Dakota S. of Mines & Tech. Pub.	1,449	211	1,868	144	217
S. Dakota S. U. Pub.	3,444	2,045	6,670	498	649
Southeastern Mass. Tech. Inst. Pub.	1,831	968	4,141	182	202
Southern C. of Optometry	336	4	346	28	34
Southern U. La. Pub.	2,375	3,562	7,232	314	345
Stevens Inst. of Tech. M	1,495	9	2,725	149	290
Tenn. A. & I. S. U. Pub.	2,230	1,925	4,543	266	287
Tenn. Tech. U. Pub.	3,477	1,626	5,944	271	396
Texas A. & M. U. Pub.	11,534	621	14,034	923*	1,025*

Institution					
Illinois Inst. of Tech.	3,037	283	8,164	316	719
Indiana Inst. of Tech.	888	4	942	40	47
Lamar S. C. of Tech. *Pub.*	4,309	2,595	8,220	325	391
Los Angeles C. of Optometry	224	7	231	13	40
Louisiana Poly. Inst. *Pub.*	4,434	2,133	7,710	385	447
Lowell Tech. Inst.	2,976	93	3,109	224	230
Maryland S. C. *Pub.*	421	216	775	58	61
Mass. Inst. of Tech.	6,915	482	8,024	1,144	1,714†
Menlo C. *M*	541	0	546	32	53
Michigan Tech. U. *Pub.*	4,111	352	4,728	295	320
Montana C. of Mineral Sc. & Tech. *Pub.*	669	183	905	49	49
Naval Postgraduate School *M Pub.*	1,498	10	1,508	250	250
N. Mex. Inst. of Mining & Tech. *Pub.*	546	119	787	58	74
Newark C. of Eng'g *Pub.*	3,000	60	4,953	286	363
Nichols C. *M*	701	0	713	38	41

Institution					
Tri-State Inst.	1,568	30	1,948	100	100
Tuskegee Inst.	1,482	1,440	3,062	235	345
U. S. Air Force Academy *M Pub.*	3,860	0	3,860	620	620
U. S. Coast Guard Academy *M Pub.*	925	0	925	114	114
U. S. Merchant Marine Academy *M Pub.*	1,014	0	1,014	88	88
U. S. Military Academy *M Pub.*	3,845	0	3,845	468	468
U. S. Naval Academy *M Pub.*	4,187	0	4,187	568	568
U. of Rhode Island *Pub.*	4,618	3,221	14,101	600	775
Va. Commonwealth U. *Pub.*	4,587	3,860	13,893	886	1,256
Va. Poly. Inst. *Pub.*	8,590	1,591	11,245	843	1,088
Webb Inst. of Naval Arch. *M*	80	0	80	8	13
West Coast U.			1,315	4	62
West Va. Inst. of Tech. *Pub.*	1,833	472	2,480	143	158
Woodbury	1,184	581	2,143	67	76
Worcester Poly. Inst. *M*	1,784	28	2,181	172	271
Totals	167,428	45,105	281,200	17,409	24,439

* Approximate
[1] 1968-69

TABLE 3
OTHER INDEPENDENT INSTITUTIONS
Teachers Colleges

Institution	Men Full-time	Women Full-time	Grand Total Students	Full-time Teaching Staff	Total Teaching Staff
Adams S. C., Colo. Pub.	1,370	1,066	2,835	135	169
Ala. S. U., Florence Pub.	1,461	1,307	3,114	134	159
Ala. S. U., Jacksonville Pub.	2,938	2,060	5,651	208	226
Ala. S. U., Livingston Pub.	1,062	416	1,775	76	102
Ala. S. U., Montgomery Pub.	760	1,133	2,340	93	103
Albany S. C. Pub.			1,816	96	115
Appalachian S. U.	2,576	2,767	6,800	295	385
Aroostook S. C.	248	305	556	32	33
Austin Peay S. U. Pub.	1,642	1,104	3,421	125	167
Ball State U. Pub.	6,188	6,973	16,664	767	855
Bank Street C. of Ed.	25	122	908	24	81
Black Hills S. C. Pub.	1,379	876	3,686	95	114
Bluefield S. C. Pub.	611	302	1,248	68	77
Brentwood W	0	79	115	11	17
Castleton S. C., Vt., Pub.	499	524	1,150	65	78
Central S. U., Ohio Pub.	1,307	1,039	2,567	120	134
Chicago S. C. Pub.	1,080	1,727	5,943	234	282
Colo. S. C. Pub.	3,766	4,773	11,682	503	578
Concord Pub.	914	979	2,019	107	110
Concordia T. C., Ill.	536	801	1,457	99	127
Concordia T. C., Nebr.	669	793	1,569	76	113
Conn. S. C., Central Pub.	2,968	3,075	10,609	352	544
Conn. S. C., Eastern Pub.	358	771	1,616	125	154
Conn. S. C., Southern Pub.	2,314	4,161	11,194	386	532

Institution	Men Full-time	Women Full-time	Grand Total Students	Full-time Teaching Staff	Total Teaching Staff
Frostburg Pub.	897	1,218	2,316	125	132
Maryland S. C., Salisbury Pub.	368	597	1,190	60	62
Maryland S. C., Towson Pub.	1,971	2,937	8,861	346	386
Mass. S. C., Boston Pub.	2,247	2,437	7,534	305	396
Mass. S. C., Bridgewater Pub.	1,051	1,954	5,773	192	215
Mass. S. C., Fitchburg Pub.	792	1,327	4,196	175	251
Mass. S. C., Framingham W Pub.	275	1,718	3,743	120	200
Mass. S. C., Lowell Pub.	438	1,341	1,779	121	136
Mass. S. C., North Adams Pub.	353	591	1,720	74	99
Mass. S. C., Salem Pub.	1,384	2,358	6,167	210	217
Mass. S. C., Westfield Pub.	686	1,401	3,425	144	158
Mass. S. C., Worcester Pub.	838	1,355	3,255	136	136
Medaille W	38	193	466	18	36
Michigan U., Northern Pub.	4,050	2,747	7,839	278	389
Minn. S. C., Bemidji Pub.	2,567	1,799	5,011	240	290
Minn. S. C., Mankato Pub.	5,920	4,653	12,635	655	873
Minn. S. C., Moorhead Pub.	2,566	2,285	5,235	274	327
Minn. S. C., St. Cloud Pub.	4,268	3,910	9,657	427	476
Minn. S. C., Winona Pub.	1,839	1,517	4,082	171	227
Miss. Valley S. C.	1,080	1,197	2,282	101	162
Missouri S. C., Northeast Pub.	2,817	2,176	6,319	216	234

Institution					
Conn. S. C., Western Pub.	770	1,383	3,605	147	173
Dakota S. C. Pub.	800	486	1,471	61	64
Delta S. C. Pub.	1,390	1,071	2,813	122	136
District of Columbia T. C. Pub.	497	984	1,911	130	166
East Carolina U. Pub.	4,298	4,676	9,687	567	717
Fairmont S. C. Pub.	1,749	1,365	3,289	157	160
George Peabody C. for T.	460	1,015	1,899	148	204
Georgia S. C., Fort Valley Pub.	838	1,175	2,247	104	104
Georgia Southern	2,420	2,534	5,178	284	309
Glenville S. C. Pub.	843	744	1,698	89	89
Grambling	1,657	1,798	3,699	174	189
Gratz	34	48	166	12	45
Harris T. C. Pub.	310	874	1,470	59	79
Hebrew T. C.	27	41	111	3	11
Henderson S. C.	1,673	1,187	3,380	150	153
Illinois U., Eastern Pub.	3,476	3,801	7,887	618	651
Illinois U., Western Pub.	5,527	4,915	11,112	580	610
Indiana S. U. Pub.	6,326	4,889	14,407	790	1,159
Indiana U. of Pennsylvania Pub.	4,421	5,213	10,233	538	601
Jackson S. C., Miss. Pub.	1,931	2,295	4,541	201	212
Jackson S. C., Vt. Pub.	325	310	691	42	53
Kansas S. T. C., Emporia Pub.	3,092	2,990	7,150	286	381
Keene S. C. Pub.	822	994	2,302	98	118
Lesley W Pub.	0	622	728	33	61
Longwood W Pub.	0	1,873	1,955	135	138
Lyndon S. C., Vt. Pub.	356	270	647	43	55
Madison Pub.	660	2,784	3,818	237	248
Maine S. C., Farmington Pub.	413	726	1,369	66	70
Maine S. C., Gorham Pub.	713	871	2,329	79	105
Mary Rogers W	6	93	129	14	34
Maryland S. C., Bowie Pub.	338	418	1,609	72	83
Maryland S. C., Coppin Pub.	274	649	1,172	58	65
Maryland S. C.,					

Institution					
Missouri S. C., Northwest Pub.	2,449	1,963	5,136	254	273
Missouri S. C., Southeast Pub.	3,393	2,941	7,132	319	342
Montana C., Eastern Pub.	1,848	1,501	3,815	144	193
Montana C., Western Pub.	611	409	1,112	47	50
Morehead S. U. Pub.	3,266	2,444	6,947	286	321
Murray S. U. Pub.	3,744	2,661	7,834	356	504
National C. of Ed.	47	543	2,023	45	103
Nebr. S.C., Chadron Pub.	1,207	810	2,332	108	123
Nebr. S.C., Kearney Pub.	2,840	2,201	5,939	233	281
Nebr. S.C., Peru Pub.	754	372	1,261	52	57
Nebr. S.C., Wayne Pub.	1,489	1,147	3,006	114	136
N. J. S. C., Glassboro Pub.	1,409	2,530	9,140	328	398
N. J. S. C., Jersey City Pub.	1,141	2,257	7,801	266	394
N. J. S. C., Montclair Pub.	1,786	2,779	9,018	315	436
N. J. S. C., Newark Pub.	1,076	2,885	11,091	300	593
N. J. S. C., Paterson Pub.	1,295	2,988	5,755	292	313
N. J. S. C., Trenton Pub.	1,379	3,173	7,036	349	499
New Mexico Highlands U. Pub.	1,304	840	2,376	105	106
North Car. S. C. Fayetteville Pub.	453	634	1,137	76	76
North Car. S. C. Winston-Salem Pub.	438	699	1,346	100	106
North Dakota S. C., Dickinson Pub.	831	709	1,582	79	86
North Dakota S. C., Mayville Pub.	537	379	924	45	49
North Dakota S. C., Minot Pub.	1,388	1,297	3,339	140	155
North Dakota S. C., Valley City Pub.	700	619	1,355	62	70
Northeastern Ill. S. C. Pub.	1,217	2,115	6,732	279	378
Northern Arizona U. Pub.	3,285	3,157	8,704	421	468
Northwestern, Iowa	353	300	708	50	55

Teachers Colleges (*Continued*)

Institution	Men Full-time	Women Full-time	Grand Total Students	Full-time Teach-ing Staff	Total Teach-ing Staff
Okla. S. C., Central *Pub.* —	4,315	2,454	10,572	293	350
Okla. S. C., East Central *Pub.*	1,416	1,151	3,003	98	122
Okla. S. C., Northeastern *Pub.*	3,276	2,430	5,776	209	238
Okla. S. C., Southeastern *Pub.*	1,237	777	2,533	121	133
Oregon C. of Ed. *Pub.*	1,583	1,890	3,688	179	209
Oregon C., Eastern *Pub.*	805	642	1,712	80	94
Oregon C., Southern *Pub.*	2,244	1,828	4,432	199†	250
Pacific Oaks	8	58	311	5	15
Pa. S. C., Blooms-burg *Pub.*	1,905	1,669	4,125	228	283
Pa. S. C., California *Pub.*	2,929	2,217	6,626	350	351
Pa. S. C., Cheyney *Pub.*	800	1,000	2,005	186	193
Pa. S. C., Clarion *Pub.*	1,588	1,867	4,037	219	250
Pa. S. C., East Stroudsburg *Pub.*	1,034	1,371	2,612	169	172
Pa. S. C., Edinboro *Pub.*	2,399	3,465	6,849	384	432
Pa. S. C., Kutztown *Pub.*	1,512	2,458	4,249	247	253
Pa. S. C., Lock Haven *Pub.*	1,038	1,276	2,360	154	157
Pa. S. C., Mansfield *Pub.*	1,119	1,701	2,877	224	224
Pa. S. C., Millers-ville *Pub.*	1,831	2,045	4,427	281	303
Pa. S. C., Shippens-burg *Pub.*	1,672	2,037	3,758	253	258
Pa. S. C., Slippery Rock *Pub.*	1,687	2,437	4,948	330	330
Pa. S. C., West Chester *Pub.*	2,327	3,468	6,742	448	481
Plymouth S. C. *Pub.*	796	1,111	2,231	103	106

Institution	Men Full-time	Women Full-time	Grand Total Students	Full-time Teach-ing Staff	Total Teach-ing Staff
Radford *W Pub.* —	0	3,544	3,959	226	226
Rhode Island C. *Pub.*	959	2,145	3,209	233	245
St. John C. of Cleveland *W*	0	522	902	68	100
Sam Houston S. C. *Pub.*	4,070	3,098	9,152	329	563
South Dakota S. C., Northern *Pub.*	1,714	1,460	3,474	133	147
South Dakota S. C., Southern *Pub.*	785	264	1,307	74	93
State C. of Arkansas *Pub.*	2,035	2,144	4,615	190	197
Stephen F. Austin S. C. *Pub.*	4,054	3,747	8,827	350	518
Sul Ross S. C. *Pub.*	1,319	642	2,304	99	135*
Teachers C., Colum-bia U.	842	1,264	5,265	223	380
Texas S. U., East	4,238	2,889	8,782	342	574
Texas S. C., South-west *Pub.*	4,472	3,954	9,372	302	395
U. of Northern Iowa *Pub.*	3,697	4,551	10,183	450	530
Wash. S. C., Central *Pub.*	3,523	3,167	6,927	367*	472*
Wash. S. C., Eastern *Pub.*	3,407	2,481	6,345	293	313
Wash. S. C., Western *Pub.*	4,286	4,079	9,942	405	426
West Liberty S. C. *Pub.*	1,729	1,399	4,047	189	207
Western Carolina U. *Pub.*	2,456	1,792	5,184	268	304
Western Kentucky U. *Pub.*	5,512	3,984	12,030	473	587
Western New Mexico U. *Pub.*	639	431	1,438	60	80
Western S. C., Colo. *Pub.*	1,852	1,141	3,647	134	137
Wheelock *W*	3	582	665	38	66
Totals	246,915	262,943	654,953	29,882	36,364

* Approximate
† Full-time equivalents

TABLE 3
OTHER INDEPENDENT INSTITUTIONS
Fine Arts, Applied Arts and Music

Institution	Men Full-time	Women Full-time	Grand Total Students	Full-time Teaching Staff	Total Teaching Staff
Art Center C. of Design, Calif.	614	139	1,199	36	99
Boston Conservatory of Music	181	233	426	29	72
Calif. C. of Arts and Crafts	615	642	1,469	69	119
Calif. Inst. of the Arts	238	166	404	79	79
Cranbrook Academy of Art	82	42	125	8	22
Juilliard School of Music	398	292	1,057	47	114
	336	166	780	39	51
Kansas City Art Inst.	480	463	998	44	81
Maryland Institute, C. of Art	245	425	670	45	45
Massachusetts C. of Art	105	64	171	17	28
Minneapolis School of Art	247	182	606	27	35
Moore C. of Art *W*	0	504	543	33	85
New England Conservatory	267	239	574	69	133
Otis Art Inst. of Los Angeles County *Pub.*	101	66	444	12	31
Peabody Conservatory of Music	184	148	455	29	77
Philadelphia C. of Art	464	522	1,676	80	146
Rhode Island School of Design	578	537	1,115	98	116
San Francisco Conservatory of Music	61	48	123	5	58
Westminster Choir C.	174	235	422	45	55
Totals	5,370	5,113	13,257	811	1,446

TABLE 3
OTHER INDEPENDENT INSTITUTIONS
Theological Seminaries and Schools for Lay Workers

Institution	Men Full-time	Women Full-time	Grand Total Students	Full-time Teaching Staff	Total Teaching Staff
Academy of the New Church	49	43	105	13	30
Aquinas Inst. of Theol.	78	5	105	17	20
Bangor Theol. Seminary	96	15	116	10	19
Bethany Bible C.	247	178	458	18	27
Cardinal Glennon Theol. *M*	211	0	211	10	29
Crozer Theol. Seminary & Foundation	95	5	115	19	32
Eastern Baptist Theol. Seminary	123	4	184	9	17
Hebrew Union— Graduate Theol. Union	146	14	167	119	119
Hebrew Union C.— Jewish Inst. of Religion, Calif.	36	4	438	6	29
Hebrew Union C.— Jewish Inst. of Religion, Ohio	214	1	282	24	47
Immaculate Conception Seminary *M*	184	0	188	25	25
Jewish Theol. Seminary of America	268	116	468	71	35
Maryknoll C., Ill. *M*	127	5	134	31	
Maryknoll Seminary, N.Y. *M*	113	0	113	14	35
Mt. Angel Seminary *M*	99	0	106	25	29
Northern Baptist					

Institution	Men Full-time	Women Full-time	Grand Total Students	Full-time Teaching Staff	Total Teaching Staff
Theol. Seminary - Notre Dame Seminary, La. *M*	47	1	66	9	14
Oblate C., D. C. *M*	119	0	129	13	34
Oblate C. of the Southwest *M*	117	0	117	17	17
Philadelphia C. of Bible	36	0	36	7	15
Presbyterian School of Christian Education	269	317	615	39	55
Princeton Theol. Seminary	32	37	100	11	11
St. Francis Seminary, Wisc. *M*	512	37	641	41	60
St. Patrick's *M*	299	0	299	23	28
St. Paul Seminary, Minn. *M*	135	0	135	17	28
Scarritt C.	134	0	146	10	12
Seminary of St. Vincent de Paul *M*	67	78	172	16	19
Simpson Bible C.	81	0	81	8	13
Union Theol. Seminary	106	103	250	15	28
University of Judaism	394	86	514	37	75
Westminster Theol. Seminary *M*	19	37	428	11	53
Woodstock C. *M*	161	0	174	12	14
	142	0	142	20	26
Totals	4,756	1,086	7,235	717	995

TABLE 4
FRESHMAN ENROLLMENTS IN 948
INSTITUTIONS
Fields: arts and sciences, engineering, business, agriculture, education, nursing, all others

| | 1968-69 | | 1969-70 | |
	Men	Women	Men	Women
Arts and Sciences	233,581	199,715	240,285	210,549
Engineering	59,554	1,293	59,300	1,594
Business	56,101	15,093	57,263	15,768
Agriculture	11,469	2,265	11,758	2,581
Education	31,488	74,522	32,376	79,192
Nursing	246	13,339	266	14,335
All Others	100,103	83,512	107,344	89,500
Totals	492,542	389,739	508,592	413,519

TABLE 5
LARGEST INSTITUTIONS
(Including component units)

	Full-time	Rank	Grand Total	Rank
State University of New York	179,107	1	286,707	1
The California State Colleges	139,100	2	265,537	2
The City University of New York	83,053	3	167,302	3
The Wisconsin State University System	54,793	4	61,890	8
University of Texas System	51,661	5	64,572	7
University of Wisconsin	50,504	6	68,109	6
University of Minnesota	50,415	7	70,234	5
University of Illinois	46,292	8	54,076	9
Ohio State University	44,560	9	49,132	13
Indiana University	41,854	10	53,575	10
Michigan State University	39,244	11	50,085	11
University of Missouri	36,427	12	47,170	15
Pennsylvania State University	35,764	13	49,859	12
University of Maryland	35,537	14	48,203	14
University of North Carolina	34,757	15	40,923	16
University of Michigan	30,225	16	38,328	17
Southern Illinois University	27,871	17	36,446	20
University of Tennessee	27,408	18	36,320	21
Purdue University	27,226	19	36,888	19
University of Washington	26,909	20	32,749	26
Louisiana State University	25,355	21	32,601	27
Brigham Young University	22,139	22	—	—
Wayne State University	21,475	23	34,924	23
Kent State University	21,166	24	28,731	29
University of Massachusetts	20,395	25	—	—
University of Cincinnati	20,107	26	35,174	22
University of Colorado	20,032	27	—	—
Rutgers—The State University	19,460	28	31,096	28
University of Florida	19,211	29	—	—
Iowa State University	18,094	30	—	—
University of California*	—	—	106,274	4
Northeastern University	—	—	37,134	18
New York University	—	—	33,421	24
Temple University	—	—	32,973	25
University of Pittsburgh	—	—	28,426	30

* Did not report full-time figures.

TABLE 6
GEOGRAPHICAL DIVISION SUMMARY
Full-time Students

Division and State	Comparable Institutions	Number of Full-time Students	
		1968-69	1969-70
(1) *New England*			
Maine	12	17,803	18,563
New Hampshire	8	16,646	17,589
Vermont	12	13,946	15,551
Massachusetts	48	142,303	149,060
Rhode Island	8	21,372	22,787
Connecticut	18	54,815	59,043
(2) *Middle Atlantic*			
New York	82	412,260	440,079
New Jersey	22	71,166	75,473
Pennsylvania	84	221,594	234,639
(3) *East North Central*			
Ohio	50	221,152	228,113
Indiana	30	130,448	133,150
Illinois	46	192,891	204,203
Michigan	29	153,123	160,205
Wisconsin	21	120,895	127,127
(4) *West North Central*			
Minnesota	24	100,061	105,129
Iowa	26	71,388	70,588
Missouri	33	88,625	93,758
North Dakota	7	18,771	20,848
South Dakota	13	22,936	23,890
Nebraska	14	37,409	37,954
Kansas	24	64,565	65,612
(5) *South Atlantic*			
Delaware	2	8,888	9,810
Maryland	22	64,899	66,650
District of Columbia	8	26,589	26,726
Virginia	26	56,918	59,171
West Virginia	16	41,704	45,193
North Carolina	31	91,505	94,323
South Carolina	17	34,944	36,641
Georgia	25	58,301	61,001
Florida	18	72,558	79,539
(6) *East South Central*			
Kentucky	21	62,849	64,604
Tennessee	31	75,247	78,892
Alabama	18	54,022	54,634
Mississippi	12	32,054	32,083
(7) *West South Central*			
Arkansas	15	41,478	41,109
Louisiana	17	82,311	85,338
Oklahoma	17	70,237	70,592
Texas	48	213,344	225,301
(8) *Mountain*			
Montana	8	20,413	21,998
Idaho	4	11,893	12,132
Wyoming	(1)	(6,804)	—
Colorado	13	55,554	60,304
New Mexico	8	26,389	28,939
Arizona	4	40,384	42,048
Utah	5	50,327	52,090
Nevada	(1)	(4,845)*	(8,031)
(9) *Pacific*			
Alaska	2	2,113	2,013
Washington	15	67,904	72,566
Oregon	16	52,974	54,436
California	55	170,782	182,268
Hawaii	3	16,991	17,171
(10) *Territorial*			
Puerto Rico	1	4,690	4,603

* Reno campus only

of today to have even a chance of meeting the challenges ahead of us in the last 30 years of the 20th century. The arts and sciences provide a mother lode of intellectual resources that can be brought to bear upon our problems only if the educative process exposes it, and if the students and professors diligently mine this precious deposit. The writer contends that this is a *sine qua non*, though not a guarantee, of success in our time. In addition, the arts and sciences provide a background of general education that is essential for the preparation of the corps of graduate and professional school trainees so necessary for the functioning of our society and economy.

Business Administration Shows Gain for Sixth Year

Freshmen in business administration, with a 2.6% increase and 73,031 students in the comparable schools, barely surpassed the 2.3% increase of 1968-69 and continued in the gain column for the sixth year in a row. The increasing complexity of American business and economic life highlights the need for the continued production of specialists in management. These may be baccalaureate-based in their professional training or they may move from a wide variety of undergraduate curricula to business specialization at the graduate level, but the need for managerial leaders continues to mount.

Engineers Are the Trailer Group—Up Only 0.1%

True to their performance record over the last decade, engineering freshmen lag behind other academic groups in enrollments for 1969-70. With 60,894 freshmen counted in the comparable schools, there was only a barely perceptible rise of 0.1%. Given the space orientation and the increasing technical complexity of our time, we may lament the fact that more young people do not choose engineering careers. Indeed, the young man or woman who has the aptitude and the application to tackle the rugged academic road laid out for the engineering student is deserving of our high encouragement and gratitude. There is some rationalizing in the profession that the low level engineering holds among the choices of students at the freshman year is, or can be, made up by transfers at the upper years or by students specializing in engineering at the graduate level. To date, the writer has not been convinced by available evidence that this is the answer. In fact, as the space industry moves toward a standardization of its techniques in interplanetary voyages and orbiting missions, the emphasis on glamor and creativity is likely to move substantially from the engineer to the pure scientist. This does not belie the continued, and even increasing, need for more engineers, but it does point up the challenge that the engineering profession, higher education as a whole, and, indeed, all of society face in encouraging qualified young people to consider engineering as a career.

All Other Freshmen Up by 7.2%

The miscellaneous "all others" category covers the academic disciples not singled out in this report series, especially the technical and vocational fields, and some of the general college curricula alluded to earlier. The fact that the 196,844 freshmen included here show an increase of 7.2% for 1969-70 has significance for all of the above-noted disciplines, as well as those not pinpointed in this study.

Full-Time Students—the Prime Group in Higher Education

The premise here is that full-time students, *i.e.*, those who devote substantially all of their working time to their studies, comprise the academic core in higher education that receives first consideration in academic, physical, and fiscal planning. Primarily, it is from this group that the nation derives its main supply of business administrators, clergymen, doctors, engineers, lawyers, nurses, teachers, other professionals, and leaders in many fields. The part-time study contingent likewise occupies a position of great importance in the educational framework, but one that generally is secondary to the full-time students.

Full-Time Students in the Large Public Universities Gain 6.8%

Always of high interest in the full-time student categories are the large public universities. With 85 schools reporting comparatively and enrolling 1,754,948 full-time students, the percentage gain for 1969-70 was 6.8%, second only to the music, fine, and applied arts schools as a group. The gain in 1968-69 was eight per cent and the year before, 7.5%. Ponderously, but inexorably, the large public universities are attracting an ever-increasing portion of the student population. In 1969-70, 44% of all full-time students in the schools surveyed enrolled in the large public universities; in 1963-64, the percentage was 37%. This trend is largely reflective of the greater financial, physical, and academic resources that are at the command of the great public universities as compared to the private schools.

Large Private Universities Up Only 2.2%

By contrast, the great private universities are falling behind in the numbers served and, perhaps, in academic, as well as fiscal, resources. The 60 comparable institutions in this group tabulated 460,675 full-time students for 1969-70, a rise of just 2.2%, a rate only slightly above the arts and sciences colleges, the lowest percentage gain group. In 1968-69, private universities had 12% of the students in the comparable institutions surveyed and about 13% for the three prior years; now, the proportion is 11.6%. In recent years, reference has been made to the blurring of the lines between public and private institutions as increasing public support was granted to private schools and the public universities gained in nonpublic financial aid. The quality education provided by the great private institutions is of high importance to the nation and deserving of continued support.

Music, Fine, and Applied Arts Up by 8.1%

In an unprecedented spurt, full-time students in 17 music, fine, and applied arts schools, with 9,747 counted, led all other school groups, with an increase of 8.1%. The sharp increase here, pursuant to a rise of 3.5% in 1968-69, perhaps is reflective of a rising interest in things cultural and, also, of an increasing application of art in the world of business and industry. Without question, many fine and applied arts schools are filled with highly qualified students.

Teachers Take Third Place in Percentage Race— Up by 6.5%

Perennially either first or second in the percentage gain column, the 144 teachers colleges with comparable data reported 500,430 enrolled full-time students, for a gain of 6.5%. In 1968-69, the gain was 8.8%, and it was 9.9% in 1967-68. These colleges continue to be fed by transfers from other curricula and from the two-year institutions. It is understood that this group includes some students who are not enrolled in teacher training programs, but the bulk of them are, and the statistics promise a welcome teacher supply in the foreseeable future.

Technological, Professional, and Related Schools Show a Rise of 4.8%

Reported for 73 comparable and specialized engineering, professional, technical, and related schools were 194,149 full-time students, an increment of 4.8%. Were it not for the lag in engineering freshmen in 1969-70 and 1968-69, the percentage rise would be higher. Enrollments in technical schools also are somewhat sluggish in their upward movement. Laggard enrollments in engineering and technical programs are significant for a nation whose economic and social system rests so solidly upon a technological base. We had best be mindful of the need for encouragement and support of education in these vital fields. In the other professional and related schools, such as business administration, the upward movement in numbers was noticeable.

Theological Schools Continue Decline in Full-Time Students

Pursuant to several loss years, it must be noted that 25 theological schools with comparable data experienced in 1969-70 a further decline of 4.7%, with 4,902 full-time students. The 854 part-time registrants, on the other hand, were up by 3.5%, but the grand total of 5,756 was down by 2.9%.

Arts and Sciences Colleges Lowest Percentage Increase—2.1%

Among all collegiate groups surveyed, it is somewhat surprising to see that the 1,060,685 full-time students in 685 comparably reporting arts and sciences colleges account only for a 2.1% increase in 1969-70. This seems inconsistent with the earlier report of a four per cent increase in freshman arts and sciences students, but there are explanatory factors. As previously indicated, some of the students in this freshman category were lumped there as general college students, perhaps erroneously, but in part because they were not always easily identifiable on a professional program basis. At the upper division level, especially, there is a transfer movement of students from arts and sciences curricula into professionally oriented programs. Finally, there is no doubt that many small private arts and sciences colleges are hard hit by the inflationary spiral of rising costs. Such accoutrements of higher education today as sophisticated computer installations, modern visual and aural instructional materials, costly research facilities, and expanded library resources make it increasingly difficult for the small arts and sciences colleges to stay abreast of the times. In addition, the keen competition in salaries for faculty and in fees for students provide further handicaps. These schools are in danger of pricing themselves out of the education market because of costs over which they have little control. For such institutions in any great number to be forced to the financial wall would be high tragedy in the educational realm. In 1968-69, these colleges enrolled 27.9% of all full-time students in comparably surveyed schools; in 1969-70, the percentage declined to 26.6%. It behooves the nation to show concern for the financial and academic welfare of these hundreds of fine colleges whose historic contribution to education has been of inestimable value.

Total Full-Time Students Advance by 4.8%

In 1,089 institutions with comparable data for 1969-70, full-time students totaled 3,985,536, an increase of 4.8%. This follows a rise of 6.2% in 1968-69, and indicates the increased responsibility annually vested in the accredited schools. Although not all were reported comparably, as was noted in the first paragraph, there were 4,156,268 students in all of the 1,145 schools surveyed for 1969-70. Although returns from other reporting agencies were unavailable at this writing, it seems likely that as many as 5,500,000, or even more, full-time degree-credit students will be reported in all of the approximately 2,500 American institutions of higher education in 1969-70.

Part-Time Students Gain 4%

The 1,386,015 part-time students tabulated for 1969-70 in 1,089 comparably reporting units increased by four per cent, barely short of the rate of rise in the full-time group. By category, the part-time enrollments and percentage increases, except where a decrease is noted, were as follows: large public universities, 616,389 (6.4%); large private universities, 239,316 (a decrease of 1.1%); arts and sciences colleges, 331,767 (.9%); technological, professional, and related schools, 60,647 (7.7%); teachers colleges, 134,391 (9.6%); fine arts, applied arts, and music, 2,651 (7.9%); and theological schools, 854 (3.5%).

Part-time students, generally, are older and more mature persons who work full-time and attend classes in the evening, late afternoon, on Saturday, and sometimes in the day. There are many motivations for part-time collegiate attendance. Among them are recreation, cultural advancement, teacher certification, degree attainment, and refresher and in-service training at both undergraduate and graduate levels. Continuing education increasingly is supported by industry via tuition remission for employees. Part-time training is a boon to students, employers, and society, and surely deserves state and Federal financial support on a credit-hour basis equal to that granted to full-time education.

Grand Total Enrollments Enlarged by 4.6%

In the 1,089 accredited and comparable institutions, the grand total enrollment for 1969-70 was 5,371,551, an increase of 4.6%. It formerly was the custom in this report to present a summary of the results of the U.S. Office of Education opening fall enrollment report. In more recent years, this data has not been available by the writing of this column, and such is the case for 1969-70. Despite that fact, it seems safe to assume that 7,750,000 or more students will be counted in the approximately 2,500 collegiate institutions in the nation. As indicated last year, partially on the basis of the calculations of Ronald B. Thompson, renowned for his precise enrollment predictions, and in reflection of other data, the author expects that we will have 10,500,000 or more college students enrolled in 1975. As indicated by Thompson, and supported by U.S. Office of Education projections, there will be a decline in the number of 18-year-olds between 1975 and 1984. This enrollment deterrent probably will be offset by the rising rate of college attendance among 18-year-olds. Collegiate enrollments undoubtedly will continue to increase through 1975, but thereafter barely may hold their own for some years. It seems unlikely, however, that there will be any enrollment decline in the 1970's.[87]

Peripheral, but important, aspects of the 1969-70 enrollments now are appropriate for consideration.

The Leaders in Size—the Big 30

The tabulation of the big 30 universities in full-time and grand total categories always is of high interest. Size is no synonym of quality, but this listing is another approach to quantification in higher education that merits attention. In former years, reference was made to the difficulties in determining this ranking. In many respects, the comparison of single-campus institutions to multi-campus statewide systems seems odd, but the fact is that such an arrangement exists and this report recognizes that situation. The author anticipates a format revision after this 50th anniversary report, and will appreciate thoughtful suggestions for changes in future studies. The top 30 schools and/or systems in 1969-70 enrolled 1,270,141 full-time students and a grand total of 1,958,859. This amounts to 30.6%[88] of the full-time students and 34.1% of all the students enrolled in the reporting and accredited institutions. In 1968-69, the figure was 31.1% for full-time students and 33.6% of the grand total.

Upper Division and Graduate Level Enrollment Implications

The massive number of lower division students enrolled in the accredited institutions, their counterparts in the unaffiliated two-year colleges, and the large base of former students who have completed their baccalaureate work all provide prospective students for upper division, graduate, and graduate professional programs. Many persons undertake work at these levels in response to financial assistance and pressure from their employers. The message here is that student loads at the upper academic levels in the future will tend to be

---

[87] Ronald B. Thompson, "College/University Enrollment Trends Shifting Toward Public Higher Education," *The College Store Journal*, December 1967/January 1968; Garland G. Parker, "Statistics of Attendance in American Universities and Colleges, 1968-69," *School & Society*, 95:58, January, 1969.

[88] The failure of the University of California to report full-time students lowers the expected percentage.

more nearly equated with those in the lower division. In the years just ahead, there are obvious implications for faculty, finance, and facilities to support these heavier class rolls.

Selective Service—Present and Future Impact

The anticipation in this column in 1968-69 that the military draft would not be a serious enrollment depressant in 1969-70 seems to have been borne out. Uncertainty prevailed through the spring and summer, but the announcement in September that graduate students enrolled in the fall quarter or semester in all probability would be permitted to complete the academic year proved to be a real magnet for potential enrollees. As in the previous year, most graduate schools had overadmitted and overawarded financial grants in anticipation of excessive cancellations. In the last weeks prior to the beginning of the fall term, however, graduate students enrolled in larger numbers than had been expected.

In view of the slowdown in the war in Vietnam, the increasing Vietnamization of the military forces there, the slackening in draft calls, and the draft lottery arrangement, it seems logical to expect a resurgence of graduate and professional enrollments in 1970-71.

Urban Enrollments Move Ahead

As urbanism gathers powerful, massive, and even dangerous momentum in American life, and as urban problems multiply and intensify, the collegiate enrollment statistics annually compiled here take on added significance. This annual study is one of the few sources, if not the only one, on enrollment statistics in urban institutions. Cities and their universities face similar crises, and the need mounts for their identification and sharing with each other in the solution of their common problems. In 89 comparably reporting members of the Association of Urban Universities, the student enrollments and increases for 1969-70 were as follows: full-time, 771,779, 6.1%; part-time, 441,398, .9%; and grand total, 1,213,177, 4.1%. All urban institutions do not belong to the association, but all members are in urban areas. Their enrollments provide significant data on higher education in our cities. It is worth noting that the full-time increase of 6.1% was larger than the 4.8% attributed to all of the comparably reporting institutions. These 89 schools registered 19.4% of the full-time students, 31.8% of the part-time group, and 22.6% of the grand total in all institutions reporting comparably. The same percentages in 1968-69 were 17.7%, 30.1%, and 20.8%. There definitely was a lag in 1968-69 in urban enrollments, compared with those in all reporting schools, apparently a reflection of the personal security concern arising from the disorders on many urban campuses in the previous year. The figures indicate some recovery of this comparative loss in 1969-70.

Education and the Sexes

The rivalry of the sexes in collegiate attendance always is of interest and importance. The trend of the last decade reflects higher percentage gains for women in most enrollment categories and is unbroken in 1969-70. At the freshman level, the 948 comparable institutions reported the enrollment of 508,592 men, a gain of 3.3%, and 413,519 women, for a striking 6.1% leap ahead. This is a larger than usual gain for women over freshman men. Men increased by 2.9% and women by 5.4% in the arts and sciences, and in education the respective increases were 2.8% and 6.3%. Rather unexpectedly, in engineering the men decreased by .4%, while the 1,594 women increased by a striking 23.3%. In the academic areas surveyed, the freshman female percentages of total freshmen were as follows: arts and sciences, 46.7%; business, 21.6%; agriculture, 18%; education, 71%; engineering, 2.6%; nursing, 98.2%; and "all others," 45.5%. Of the freshman total enrollment, women comprised 44.8%; in 1968-69, the proportion was 44%.

In the full-time category, for 1969-70, there were 1,617,358 women and 2,368,178 men, for respective gains of 5.5% and 4.3%. The female percentages in each institutional category were as follows: large public universities, 39%; large private universities, 32.1%; arts and sciences colleges, 45.6%; teachers colleges, 51.2%; technological, professional, and related colleges, 20.1%; music, fine arts, and applied arts, 49.2%; and theological schools, 18.3%. Of all full-time students, women comprised 40.6%, as compared to 40.2% in 1968-69.

Much attention was given in 1968-69 to the trend away from separate colleges for men and women and toward coeducation. The fact is that the trend continues, with institutions such as Yale University, Kenyon College, Princeton University, Xavier University, and the University of San Diego joining the coeducational parade.

As the preliminary survey for this report showed in October, 1969, however, many men's and women's colleges that returned early questionnaires showed real numerical strength in their enrollments. In women's colleges, freshman enrollment increases were reported by 47 schools, decreases by 26, and no change by 13. In total enrollments, the respective counts were 33, 38, and 15. Men's colleges did not fare quite so well. Twenty-two had freshman increases, 20 had decreases, and 13 indicated no change. In total enrollments, 19 men's colleges experienced increases, 23 had decreases, and 13 were unchanged. Again, this annual report is one of the few data sources on enrollments in separate-sex colleges.

Geographical Spread of Enrollments

Table 6 reflects geographical enrollments for 1969-70 on a regional basis. The full-time student counts are as follows: New England, 282,593 (5.9% increase); Middle Atlantic, 750,191 (6.4% increase); East North Central, 852,798 (4.2% increase); West North Central, 417,779 (3.5% increase); South Atlantic, 479,054 (5% increase); East South Central, 230,213 (2.7% increase); West South Central, 422,340 (3.7% increase); Mountain, 217,511 (6.1% increase); Pacific, 328,454 (5.7% increase); and Puerto Rico, 4,603 (1.9% decrease). The area with the highest percentage gain was the Middle Atlantic region, with 6.4%, and the lowest in the 50 states was the East South Central, with 2.7%. The nonreporting of the University of Puerto Rico and the University of Wyoming affected the validity of the regional data for 1969-70.

Veteran Enrollments Veer Upward

Basic data on veteran enrollments were provided by Edwin Williams, assistant director, Veterans Administration Information Service, as of Oct. 31, 1969. Under Chapter 31, Title 38, Veterans Benefits, U.S. Code (which includes former Public Law 892—Korean Vocational Rehabilitation and Public Law 87-815—Peacetime Vocational Rehabilitation), 8,379 college-level veterans were enrolled, an increase of 73.2%. The Orphans Education program, under Chapter 35, U.S. Code, Title 38 (formerly Public Law 634—Orphan Education), had 22,370 registrants, a growth of 5.1% over 1968-69.

The big number of veterans and servicemen were enrolled in

collegiate programs under Public Law 89-358 (Veterans Readjustment Benefits Act of 1966) and an amendment entitled Public Law 90-77 (Veterans Pension and Readjustment Assistance Act of 1967), effective Oct. 1, 1967, popularly known as the Vietnam or Post-Korean Era GI Bill. There were 329,826 veterans and 6,691 servicemen enrolled in collegiate programs—a total of 336,517, for a significant increase of 28.8%. The total collegiate enrollment of all veterans, servicemen, and orphans under all of the above laws was 367,266, as compared to 287,461 on Oct. 31, 1968, an increase of 27.8%.

With Vietnam demobilization a more imminent factor in the future, an even larger enrollment of veterans may be expected in 1970-71 and thereafter. Even so, available data do not indicate the veterans are seeking higher education in adequate or anticipated numbers. Pertinent factors may be the marginal academic qualifications of many draftees, the antipathy of many to the higher education establishment on a racial basis, and, on the other hand, the fact that a significant percentage of servicemen had completed their collegiate work before enlisting or being drafted. Nevertheless, the racial flare-ups on military bases in this country, as well as the reports of similar strife among servicemen in Vietnam, add urgency to the need for directing and counseling as many veterans as possible into constructive educational channels. The energies, experience, ideas, and leadership of these men can be crucial in the solution of the manifold problems facing the nation. Many will need collegiate training to prepare them for the significant role they should play in the interest of the nation and themselves. It would be high tragedy for any of these men to adapt battlefield strategies to the waging of internal conflicts on a guerrilla or underground basis. There are many Federal and institutional programs designed for the counseling and recruitment of veteran students, but there is insufficient evidence of any great involvement on the part of collegiate institutions generally with veteran students. Early counseling, vigorous recruiting, especially designed and perhaps accelerated academic programs, and adequate student, as well as program, funding are high priorities in the education of veterans. Much attention appropriately was given to the education of World War II and Korean veterans; the need for similar or even greater concern for veterans of the Vietnam conflict is clamant.

Professors Who Teach

A determined effort is made to gather viable teacher data each year, but fewer tasks are more difficult. There is great interest in the statistical output, but so many are shy about providing the data input. The information collection and analysis is complicated, of course, by the fact that there is no consensus on the definition of teachers, teaching, credit-hour loads, and the like. Some institutions tabulate only full-time teacher equivalents, and others appear not to know or choose not to report their teacher statistics. Gratitude is extended, however, to the overwhelming majority of institutional representatives that faithfully report their pedagogical data as accurately as possible.

A basic assumption is that teacher statistics primarily should reflect only those who teach. This in no wise is to denigrate full-time service in research, administration, or other professional nonteaching commitments, but teacher-student ratios should be related to those engaged in actual teaching. If dissident and other concerned students today are speaking to their institutions in support of better teaching, as well as on other issues—as this writer thinks they are—there should be a high priority upon their receiving a respectful and responsible hearing. When quality teaching is an issue, a tabulation that enumerates full-time and part-time teachers must be relevant. The teacher definitions here require that one should spend half or more of his time in instruction to be counted as a full-time teacher; others are part-time, and those not teaching should not be reported.

The reader is cautioned, however, to use the teacher statistics with much care. Varying local circumstances should be appraised before determining student-teacher ratios. A school that runs a cooperative education or professional practice program, for example, may have half or more of its students out of classes and on work sections at any given time. There are other discrepancies that creep into the teacher reports, and the full-time and grand totals should be used with care. Nevertheless, the tabulations merit careful consideration and should have value in relation to retaining, recruiting, and supervising college teachers. The teacher statistics are in Tables 1-3.

Two-Year College Movement Gains Momentum[89]

Space and limited resources precluded the gathering of complete data on enrollments in the two-year junior and community colleges for the collegiate enrollment report published in January, 1970. The opening fall enrollment report of the U.S. Office of Education separately identifies two-year college enrollments, but information from that study for 1969 was unavailable at this writing. The USOE report for 1968, however, showed a count of 1,796,426 students in all two-year institutions.[90]

Thanks have been extended over many years to the American Association of Junior Colleges for sample data indicative of significant trends in enrollment and academic developments in this increasingly important segment of higher education. We are grateful to William A. Harper, director of public relations of that organization, for such statistics as were available on Dec. 12, 1969. Junior and community college enrollments, consistent with their previous performance in the 1960's, in 1969-70 showed a 15-20% increase. About 1,060 two-year colleges had approximately 2,250,000 students on their rolls, as compared to 1,954,116 in 1968-69, an increase of 15.1%. Of these, an estimated 150,000 were in private junior colleges. New two-year colleges in 1969 numbered about 40, noticeably fewer than the 120 in 1968.

The estimate in this report in 1968-69 was that, by 1975, 50% or more of all freshmen would be enrolled in two-year colleges. The experience in Michigan for 1969-70 indicates that already 49% of all first-time collegians there were enrolled in community colleges. The new Wayne County Community College, operating in 18 Detroit centers, registered 7,886 students. Enrollments in certain other states for 1969 and 1968 (in parentheses), with percentage increases, are as follows: California, 665,490 (603,096), 10.3%; Florida, 130,669 (92,691), 41.0%; Illinois, 137,250 (102,575), 33.8%; Maryland, 36,784 (28,224), 30.3%; New York, 169,446 (154,930), 9.4%; and Virginia, 24,624 (19,030), 29.4%.

For the last 10 years, this writer has emphasized the rapid growth, significance, and the mounting mission of the two-year colleges in this country. It is of interest that such emphasis in late 1969 was corroborated and enlarged upon by James E. Allen, Jr., then U.S. Commissioner of Education. In addressing the National Council of

---

[89] Reprinted from Garland G. Parker, "Supplementary Report on Collegiate Enrollments for 1969-70," *School & Society*, 98:2323, February, 1970.

[90] Marjorie O. Chandler, *Opening Fall Enrollment in Higher Education, 1968: Part A—Summary Data* (Washington, D.C.: U.S. Government Printing Office, 1969), p. 12.

State Directors of Community-Junior Colleges, he anticipated legislation that would aid community colleges, ". . . first, by direct aid to colleges improving their career education programs, particularly as they expand opportunities for the disadvantaged, and, secondly, by aid to the states in improving their management of career education."[91]

Belated Reports

Institutions reporting too late for inclusion in the 50th anniversary report, published in the January, 1970, issue of *School & Society,* were as follows: Alliance C., f.t. 597, g.t. 604; Central Missouri State C., f.t. 9,307, g.t. 12,168; The C. of Insurance, f.t. 278, g.t. 1,600; C. of the Holy Cross, f.t. 2,505, g.t. 2,590; C. of the San Francisco Art Institute, f.t. 515, g.t. 884; Elizabeth City State U., f.t. 940, g.t. 1,039; Ferris State C., f.t. 8,267, g.t. 8,439; Finch C., f.t. 413, g.t. 416; Florida Memorial C., f.t. 819, g.t. 876; Gallaudet C., f.t. 747, g.t. 789; George Williams C., f.t. 648, g.t. 837; Manhattan School of Music, f.t. 665, g.t. 769; New Haven C., f.t. 2,283, g.t. 4,257; Northern Montana C., f.t. 1,297, g.t. 1,590; Philadelphia C. of Textiles and Science, f.t. 1,278, g.t. 1,858; St. Paul's C., D.C., f.t. 124, g.t. 129; The School of The Art Institute of Chicago, f.t. 718, g.t. 1,131; Southern Colorado State C., f.t 4,653, g.t. 5,769; Southern Utah State C., f.t. 1,593, g.t. 1,761; University of California (all campuses), f.t. 99,399 (grand total figures for the University of California were reported in the January, 1970, issue of *School & Society*); University of Puerto Rico, f.t. 27,672, g.t. 37,839; University of San Francisco, f.t. 4,178, g.t. 6,804; West Georgia C., f.t. 4,124, g.t. 5,049. These supplementary statistics raised the number of reporting schools to 1,167, with 4,329,-288 full-time students and a grand total of 5,841,533 enrollees.

[91] "Finch, Allen Give Views on Continuing Education and Community Colleges," *Higher Education and National Affairs,* 18:42, Dec. 5, 1969, p. 6.

✦ BIBLIOGRAPHY

In addition to the works cited in the footnotes, other helpful and pertinent references are listed here.

Altman, Robert A. *The Upper Division College.* San Francisco: Jossey-Bass, 1970. History, present status, and promise of the upper-division college as the capstone of the public education system through the baccalaureate.

Annual Report of the American College Testing Program for 1969-70. Iowa City, Iowa: American College Testing Program, 1970. Contains succinct survey of trends in higher education in 1969-70.

Annual Report of the American College Testing Program, 1968-69. Iowa City, Iowa: American College Testing Program, 1969. Pp. 6-17. Good summary of then current trends in higher education.

American Council on Education. *Campus Tensions: Analysis and Recommendations.* Report of the Special Committee on Campus Tensions; Sol. M. Linowitz, Chairman. Washington, D.C.: American Council on Education, 1970. A concise and penetrating report with constructive recommendations.

American Society for Engineering Education. *The Application of Technology to Education.* Washington, D.C., 1969. A brief balanced study of the application of technology to education.

Axelrod, Joseph, and Freedman, Mervin B., eds. *Search for Rele-*

vance: The Campus Crisis. San Francisco: Jossey-Bass, 1969. Focus on issues and answers to campus problems; thesis is that curricular reform is the proper approach to improvement of campus conditions.

Barzun, Jacques. *The American University: How It Runs? Where It Is Going?* New York: Harper & Row, 1968. Philosophical and practical analysis of the anatomy and operation of a university and what the future may be for it.

Bonner, Thomas N. *Our Recent Past: American Civilization in the Twentieth Century.* Englewood Cliffs, N.J.: Prentice-Hall, 1963. A comprehensive, interpretive, intellectually-oriented, general account that provides helpful background information.

Booth, Wayne C., ed. *The Knowledge Most Worth Having.* Chicago: University of Chicago Press, 1967. States a strong case for liberal education.

Brickman, William W., and Lehrer, Stanley, eds. *Automation, Education, and Human Values.* New York: School & Society Books, 1965. A series of stimulating essays that indicate the impact of technology on human life in general.

Brickman, William W., and Lehrer, Stanley, eds. *A Century of Higher Education: Classical Citadel to Collegiate Colossus.* New York: Society for the Advancement of Education, 1962. Fourteen chapters by different authors that give scholarly overviews of 100 years on various topics related to higher education.

Brickman, William W., and Lehrer, Stanley, eds. *Conflict and Change on the Campus: The Response to Student Hyperactivism.* New York, School & Society Books, 1970. Helpful analyses of student unrest, suggested solutions, and source documents.

Brubacher, John S., and Rudy, Willis. *Higher Education in Transition: A History of American Colleges and Universities, 1636-1968.* New York: Harper & Row, revised ed., 1969. A revision of a work that first appeared in 1958 and one of the best studies in print of the history of higher education in the U.S.

Califano, Joseph A. *The Student Revolution: A Global Confrontation.* New York: W. W. Norton, 1969. Study of student unrest based on world trip. Relates unrest abroad to that in the U.S.

Chickering, Arthur W. *Education and Identity.* San Francisco: Jossey-Bass, 1969. Emphasis upon personalization in higher education and means to achieve it.

College Admissions Policies for the 1970's. New York: College Entrance Examination Board, 1968. Collection of papers delivered at the Colloquium on College Admissions Policies at Interlochen, Mich., in 1967. Penetrating and helpful analysis of admissions considerations for the 1970's.

Cremin, Lawrence A. *The Transformation of the School: Progressivism in American Education, 1876-1957.* New York: Knopf, 1961. A study of the progressive education movement in historical perspective that is a major contribution to the history of American education.

Curti, Merle, and Nash, Roderick. *Philanthropy in the Shaping of American Higher Education.* New Brunswick, N.J.: Rutgers University Press, 1965. An excellent appraisal of the history and impact of philanthropy upon higher education in the U.S.

Dennis, Lawrence E., and Kauffman, Joseph F. *The College and the Student.* Washington, D.C.: American Council on Education, 1966. Forty-six essays that provide an analysis of the college student, the environment of higher education, and the responsibilities of the college and the student for coping with change in civilization.

Department of Defense. *Report of the Special Committee on ROTC to the Secretary of Defense.* Washington, D.C., 1969. Informative and sympathetic analysis of the history, role, problems of, and recommendations for ROTC programs.

Dressel, Paul L.; Johnson, Craig; and Marcus, Philip M. *The Confidence Crisis.* San Francisco: Jossey-Bass, 1970. A detailed analysis of departmental structure, how it developed, and how it may be evaluated in higher education.

Feldman, Kenneth A., and Newcomb, Theodore M. *The Impact of College on Students,* vols. 1 & 2. San Francisco: Jossey-Bass, 1969. Survey of findings in almost 1,500 reports over the past 40 years. Helpful compendium of research on higher education and college students.

Foote, Caleb; Mayer, Henry; and Associates. *The Culture of the University: Governance and Education.* San Francisco: Jossey-Bass, 1968. Report of faculty-student Study Commission on University Governance at the University of California, Berkeley. Special reference to student participation in governance.

Gaff, Jerry G., & Associates. *The Cluster College.* San Francisco: Jossey-Bass, 1970. An analytical study of the cluster concept as an effort to establish a greater sense of community and personalization in higher education.

Gardner, John W. *Excellence: Can We Be Equal And Excellent Too?* New York: Harper & Row, 1961. A good analysis of the sorting out process in higher education and need for appropriate training for all.

Gardner, John W. *The Recovery of Confidence.* New York: W. W. Norton, 1970. Perceptive analysis of society, challenges, changes, dissent, loss of confidence, problem of continuous renewal, leadership, and national agenda for the future.

Hanson, Harlan P., Director, The Four-School Study Committee. *16-20: The Liberal Education of an Age Group.* New York: College Entrance Examination Board, 1970. Intriguing study by representatives of four prestigious private preparatory schools and the College Entrance Examination Board that favors the establishment of an Intermediate College institution to comprehend the traditional last two years of secondary school and the first two years of college.

Harcleroad, Fred F., ed. *Issues of the Seventies.* Iowa City, Iowa: American College Testing Program, 1970. Edited papers presented at 1969 educational conference in Iowa City; stimulating and controversial.

Hefferlin, J. B. Lon. *Dynamics of Academic Reform.* San Francisco: Jossey-Bass, 1969. Results of a five-year study on institutional vitality, the adaptability to new conditions, and the mechanics of change in higher education.

Hofstadter, Richard. *Anti-intellectualism in American Life.* New York: Knopf, 1963. An able historian's keen but controversial analysis of the facets of anti-intellectualism in our society.

Hofstadter, Richard, and Hardy, C. De Witt. *The Development and Scope of Higher Education in the United States.* New York: Columbia University Press, 1952. Relation of higher education to its background for development and the service it renders to society.

Hofstadter, Richard, and Smith, Wilson, eds. *American Higher Education: A Documentary History,* vols. 1 & 2. Chicago: University of Chicago Press, 1961. An excellent source-book collection of documents from 1636 to 1948.

Klotsche, J. Martin. *The Urban University.* New York: Harper & Row, 1966. Role and responsibility of urban universities and an optimistic view of the future of urban life and education.

Knight, Edgar W. *Fifty Years of American Education.* New York: Ronald, 1952. A good history of education in the U.S. in the first half of the 20th century.

Knowles, Malcolm S. *Higher Adult Education in the United States.* Washington D.C.: American Council on Education, 1969. An excellent report prepared for the Committee on Higher Adult Education of the American Council on Education that reflected the current situation, trends, and issues in 1969.

Lee, Calvin B. T., ed. *Improving College Teaching.* Washington, D.C.: American Council on Education, 1967. Analysis of teaching, the academic community, academic people, teaching and learning processes, teaching innovations, evaluation of teaching, and means for improvement.

Lehrer, Stanley, ed. *Leaders, Teachers, and Learners in Academe: Partners in the Educational Process.* New York: Appleton-Century-Crofts, 1970. Compendium of over 100 valuable and scholarly essays on higher education.

Lipset, Seymour M., and Wolin, Sheldon S., eds. *The Berkeley Student Revolt: Facts and Interpretations.* Garden City, N.Y.: Doubleday, 1965. An analysis of the student revolt as it looked to several perceptive professors from the inside of the University of California at Berkeley.

Martin, Warren Bryan. *Conformity: Standards and Change in Higher Education.* San Francisco: Jossey-Bass, 1969. A study of goals in higher education, the means to attain them, and the need for reexamination of both.

Morgan, Gordon D. *The Ghetto College Student: A Descriptive Essay on College Youth from the Inner City.* Iowa City, Iowa: American College Testing Program, 1970. An account based on interviews, impressions, and anecdotes reflective of the views of the ghetto student toward college and the challenge he poses to the colleges.

Niblett, W. R., ed. *Higher Education: Demand and Response.* San Francisco: Jossey-Bass, 1970. Articulate expositions of historical and contemporary problems in higher education.

Nicholas, David C., and Mills, Olive, eds. *The Campus and the Racial Crisis.* Washington, D.C.: American Council on Education, 1970. Forty-four papers by concerned and informed persons that reflect respect for higher education and the assumption that problems will be solved.

Rogers, Carl R. *Freedom to Learn.* Columbus, Ohio: Charles E. Merrill Publishing Company, 1969. The theory of learning, the meaning of "freedom," and suggested practical approaches to improve learning.

Rudolph, Frederick. *The American College and University: A History.* New York: Knopf, 1962. An historical overview of American higher education. Inadequate for teachers colleges and junior colleges but helpful treatment of colleges and the rise of the university.

Runkel, Philip; Harrison, Roger; and Runkel, Margaret, eds. *The Changing College Classroom.* San Francisco: Jossey-Bass, 1969. Constructive approach to the improvement of teaching and learning in the college classroom.

Sampson, Edward E.; Korn, Harold A.; and Associates. *Student Activism and Protest.* San Francisco: Jossey-Bass, 1970. Timely exploration of many facets of student unrest movement in the 1960's.

Schmidt, George P. *The Liberal Arts College: A Chapter in American Cultural History.* New Brunswick, N.J.: Rutgers University Press, 1957. A good topical treatment of various aspects of development of the liberal arts colleges in the U.S.

Smith, G. Kerry, ed. *Agony and Promise: Current Issues in Higher Education, 1969.* San Francisco: Jossey-Bass, 1969. A collection of thoughtful and provocative essays on various aspects of higher education published by the American Association for Higher Education.

Smith, G. Kerry, ed. *Stress and Campus Response.* San Francisco: Jossey-Bass, 1968. Twenty-five essays presented at an annual conference of the American Association for Higher Education. Critical examination of pressing problems in higher education.

Smith, G. Kerry, ed. *Twenty-Five Years, 1945-1970.* San Francisco: Jossey-Bass, 1970. Essays collected from yearbooks of the American Association for Higher Education that are reflective of the issues in higher education in the 25 years under review.

Thomas, Russell. *The Search for a Common Learning: General Education, 1800-1960.* New York: McGraw-Hill, 1962. A good history of and defense of general education in the U.S.

Welter, Rush. *Popular Education and Democratic Thought in America.* New York: Columbia University Press, 1962. A study of the relation between democracy and education in U.S. History—thoughtful and provocative.

Wilson, Logan. *Emerging Patterns in American Higher Education.* Washington, D.C.: American Council on Higher Education, 1965. Descriptions by 34 educational leaders of changes in patterns of organization and administration with a view to strengthening higher education.

PERIODICAL REFERENCES

"Campus 1980," *College Management,* January, 1970, pp. 11-44. A series of brief articles touching upon numerous issues pertaining to higher education in the 1970's.

"The Embattled University," *Daedalus: Journal of the American Academy of Arts and Sciences,* 99:1, Winter, 1970. An analysis of university problems characterized by insight, depth, perspective, and original ideas.

INDEX